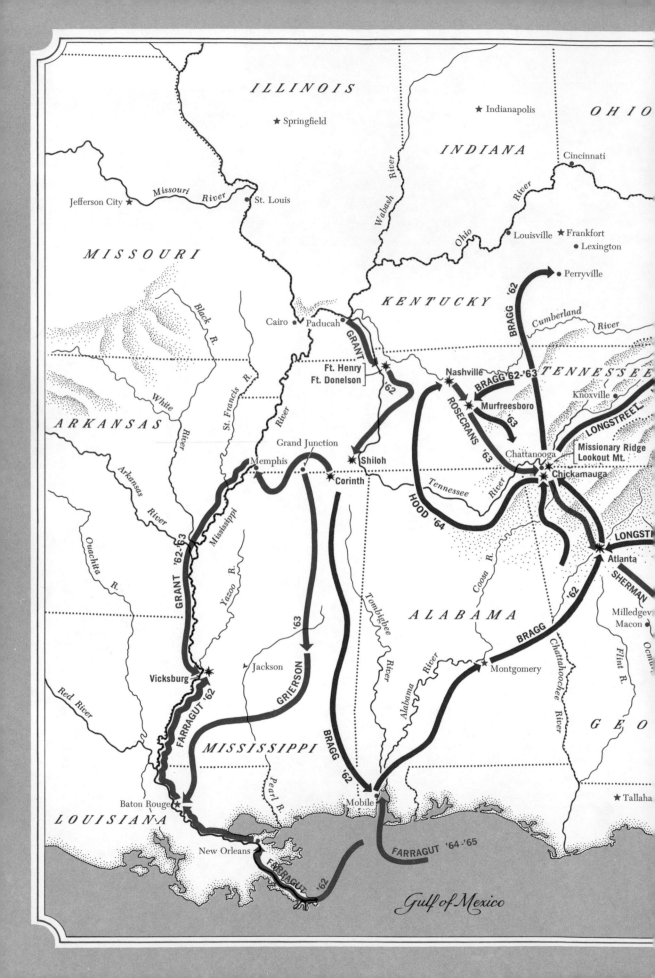

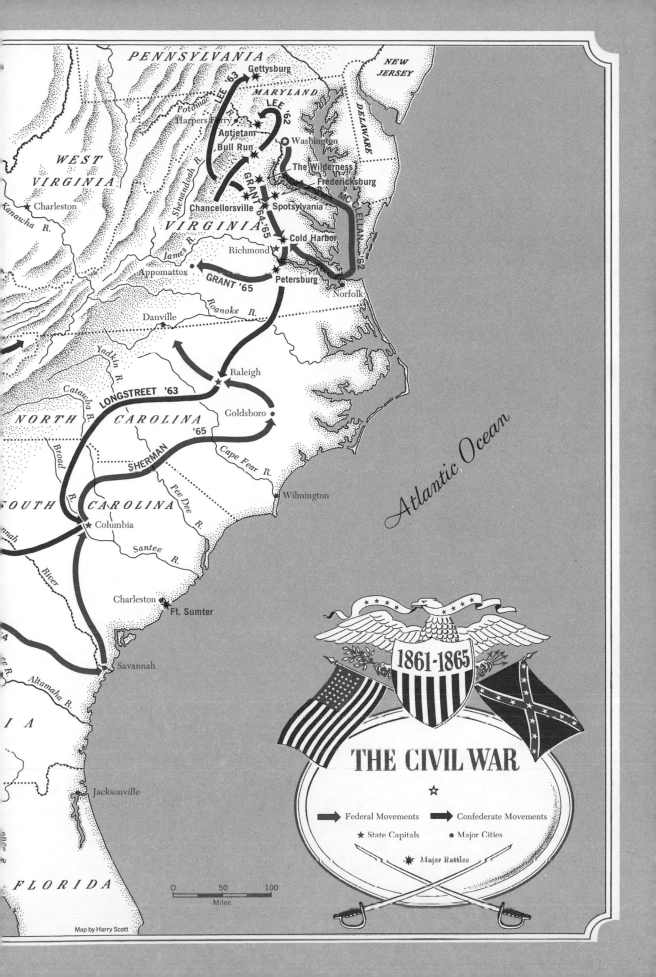

PENNSYLVANIA

NEW
JERSEY

Gettysburg

LEE '63

MARYLAND

LEE '62

DELAWARE

Potomac R.

WEST
VIRGINIA

Harpers Ferry

Antietam

Washington

Bull Run

Charleston

The Wilderness

Kanawha
R.

Shenandoah R.

GRANT
'64-'65

Fredericksburg

MC CLELLAN '62

Chancellorsville

Spotsylvania

VIRGINIA

James R.

Richmond

Cold Harbor

Appomattox

GRANT '65

Petersburg

Norfolk

Roanoke R.

Danville

Yadkin R.

Raleigh

Catawba R.

LONGSTREET '63

NORTH   CAROLINA

Goldsboro

'65

Broad R.

SHERMAN

Cape Fear R.

Atlantic Ocean

SOUTH   CAROLINA

Pee Dee R.

Wilmington

Columbia

Santee
R.

nah

River

Charleston

Ft. Sumter

'4

Savannah

Altamaha R.

1861-1865

I A

THE CIVIL WAR

☆

Jacksonville

→ Federal Movements   → Confederate Movements

★ State Capitals   ● Major Cities

✸ Major Battles

FLORIDA

0   50   100
Miles

Map by Harry Scott

A Pictorial History of
THE CIVIL WAR YEARS

A PICTORIAL HISTORY OF

THE

Civil War

YEARS

★ ★ ★ ★ ★ ★ ★ ★

By PAUL M. ANGLE

Introduction by William C. Davis

DOUBLEDAY & COMPANY, INC.   GARDEN CITY, NEW YORK

To the Memory of
Charles L. Sherman,
friend of many years,
who suggested
that I do this book.

COPYRIGHT © 1967, 1980 BY NELSON DOUBLEDAY, INC.
All rights reserved

LIBRARY OF CONGRESS CATALOG CARD NO. 84-24678

9 8 7 6 5 4 3 2 1

Library of Congress Cataloging in Publication Data

Angle, Paul McClelland
A pictorial history of the Civil War years.

Includes index.
1. United States—History—Civil War, 1861-1865. I. Title.
[E468.A56 1985]   973.7   84-24678

ISBN 0-385-18551-0 (pbk.)

INTRODUCTION

SURELY few tasks can be more difficult or demanding than trying to capture in the text of a single volume the broad sweep and complex nature of the American Civil War, particularly in a book of the relative brevity of *A Pictorial History of the Civil War Years*. Yet that is exactly what Paul Angle did—with impressive results. He captured not only the chief events of the war, but also the more subtle or obscure nuances of the times that helped make this war and its people much more complicated than they seem at first glance.

Angle was aided in his task by his skillful melding of words and illustrations. These pictures are worth thousands of words. Rather than being merely repetitious, as is so often the case, the illustrations pick up where the narrative halts, offering a graceful natural continuation and expansion of the text.

Of particular interest is Angle's treatment of the events leading up to the start of the Civil War. Many volumes have been written—and will continue to appear—attempting to explain how the war took place. The result is a sort of overkill for the average reader. In this book the author presents a broad overview which, supplemented and vividly expanded by the illustrations—particularly in the section on secession—offers as clear a picture as one could wish for general background.

Undeniably one of the chief reasons for the enduring interest in the American Civil War is the pictorial record that the people of that time left behind for us. More particularly, the photograph, itself an infant technology, provides a vitally realistic image of the young nation at war with itself which the drawings and etchings, with their artificial pose and polish, cannot. Even better than words, these pictures bring modern America as close to its past as one century can get to another.

The greatest service that the late Paul Angle did in putting this book together was to take full advantage for the first time of the pictorial treasures in the Chicago Historical Society's collections. There are several great collections of Civil War photographs in the country, some running into the tens of thousands of images. By comparison, Chicago's collection is small, just over one thousand photographs. Qualitatively it is probably, picture for picture, the best in the country. There are scores of unique rarities there, and many appear in the pages of this book.

More than twenty other archives and libraries across the land are also represented in this book. The final product is a volume that even over the years still stands high in its genre. Paul Angle, by his own admission, never intended to become a historian. Yet it is as a historian that he will be known to posterity, not only for this book but for a host of other books dealing with Lincoln and the Civil War. All bore the same mark that he impressed on this volume—a desire to make the dramatic and tragic story of the nation's most troubled era come alive for Americans of today.

Making the journey in these pages from Bull Run to Appomattox, in the company of Lee and Lincoln and Grant and Stonewall Jackson and the hundreds of thousands of ordinary Americans who lived during the Civil War, the reader can hardly fail to arrive at the conclusion that Paul Angle fulfilled his desire. It is a grand journey, a monument not only to the author, but also to those embattled and confused travelers who first made that journey over a century ago.

As in any art, history is not a static or entirely precise discipline. Work continues, new information is unearthed, and former truths are found to be in error. Serious study of Civil War photos only came of age in the 1970s, and this reissue of *A Pictorial History of the Civil War Years* has benefited from this new work. The text has been revised to reflect new research and findings; many illustrations given erroneous identification in the first edition now stand corrected. The result is not by any means a new book. Rather, a good book has been made better. In the fluid art of history this is the best we can ask.

William C. Davis

Mechanicsburg, Pennsylvania

FOREWORD

THIS BOOK is based on several premises. The first is my belief that the person who is interested in a Civil War picture book wants a book that is devoted primarily to pictures. Many readers may prefer the comprehensive text of Bruce Catton, Allan Nevins, James Ford Rhodes, or Nicolay and Hay, to name only a few of those who have told the story of this great American conflict in full detail. With them I have no quarrel. However, in accordance with my conviction I have held my text to a minimum and emphasized the story as pictures tell it.

My second premise is that the picture story should be realistic. This means reliance, first, upon the camera. But the Civil War photographers, wonderful as they were, had one deficiency. They could show bloated bodies after a battle, but with their slow lenses they could not catch a cavalry charge or an infantry attack. For action, one must rely upon the artists who accompanied the armies. In pen and ink sketches, in wash drawings, and even in oils, they caught aspects of the war that the photographers could not record.

My third premise is that the work of the artists deserves to be used in its original state. Most of them sent their drawings, often unfinished, to such publications as *Leslie's* and *Harper's,* where

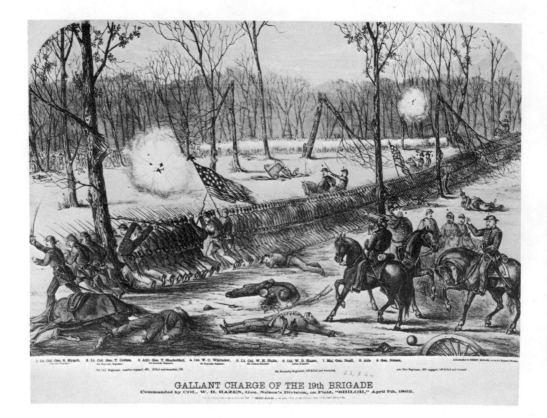

GALLANT CHARGE OF THE 19th BRIGADE
Commanded by COL. W. B. HAZEN, Gen. Nelson's Division, on Field, "SHILOH," April 7th, 1862.

engravers or lithographers turned them into their conception of what readers wanted to see. And what these conventional craftsmen did to honest pictorial reporting was criminal. The worst example I have seen is the lithograph, by Henry Mosler of *Harper's Weekly,* shown here. It is supposed to represent the charge of the 19th Brigade (Union) at the battle of Shiloh, but anyone who has ever read three hundred words about that conflict will know that nothing of the kind pictured here could have taken place on that confused and bloody field.

I have made no attempt to identify the men who took the photographs I have used. Accurate identification is impossible. Every photographer had assistants in the field, and the stamp of Brady, Gardner, or Barnard on a print is no assurance that that photographer snapped the shutter. On the other hand, the artists almost always signed their drawings, so I have taken pains to give them the credit that is their due.

Except for the seals, the sketches used in the margins come from two sources: John D. Billings's *Hardtack and Coffee, or The Unwritten Story of Army Life* (Boston, 1888), illustrated by Charles W.

Reed of the 9th Massachusetts Battery; and the southern song book *Southern War Songs: Campfire, Patriotic, and Sentimental* (New York, 1890), published by M. T. Richardson & Company, edited by William Long Fagan, and illustrated by H. D. Nichols. The work of the two artists is readily distinguishable. Reed's drawings are bold and simple; those of the illustrator of the southern song book are much more delicate.

In the making of this book I have incurred many obligations. My first debt, of course, is to those custodians of picture collections who searched their files and permitted their holdings to be reproduced. But I should be remiss if I did not acknowledge my especial indebtedness to Miss Margery Melgaard, whose extraordinary skill as a stenographer and typist greatly expedited the completion of this book; to Mrs. Paul H. Rhymer, curator of prints and photographs at the Chicago Historical Society, who constantly amazes me by her knowledge of the thousands of pictures in her custody; to Walter W. Krutz, the Chicago Historical Society's staff photographer, a craftsman without a superior; and to C. Earl Cooley, of Doubleday & Company, who was indefatigable in finding pictures in libraries and archives to which I did not have ready access.

PAUL M. ANGLE

Chicago Historical Society

NOMENCLATURE

IN MANY INSTANCES Northern and Southern historians have affixed different names to the same battle. Several of the engagements referred to or described in this book have dual names. Thus:

FEDERAL	CONFEDERATE
Antietam	Sharpsburg
Bull Run	Manassas
Second Bull Run	Second Manassas
Pea Ridge	Elkhorn Tavern
Perryville	Chaplin Hills
Shiloh	Pittsburgh Landing

The *Merrimack,* frequently misspelled *Merrimac,* raised after the destruction of the Norfolk Navy Yard and clad with iron, was renamed the *Virginia* by the Confederate Navy Department. Most writers have preferred the original name, probably because of its alliterative appeal when coupled with the *Monitor.*

Another source of confusion arises from the almost identical names of the two principal Western armies: the Union Army of the Tennessee and the Confederate Army of Tennessee. The Union army was named for the river, the Confederate army for the state.

P.M.A.

CONTENTS

A Pictorial History of
THE CIVIL WAR YEARS

THE LONG ROAD
TO SECESSION

OCTOBER comes to South Carolina as a blessed interlude between hot summer and chill and rainy winter. In the tenth month of the year the skies are blue, the breezes warm, the flowers still verdant. But in October, 1860, the amenity of nature did not soften the hard resolution of William Henry Gist, governor of the state. For years this fifty-three-year-old man who had divided his life between politics, his plantation, and the Methodist Church had been determined that the South should set itself up as an independent nation. On the fifth day of the month, in somnolent and lovely Columbia, capital of the state, he sat at his desk to write a letter to the several governors of the Cotton States. To each he predicted that Abraham Lincoln would be elected to the Presidency of the United States. This event would call for decisive action. Gist preferred that some state other than South Carolina should take the lead in seceding from the Union, but if none would, South Carolina would act alone. "If you decide to call a convention upon the election of a majority of electors favorable to Lincoln, I desire to know the day you propose for the meeting, that we may call our convention to meet the same day, if possible."

Gist's assessment of the political scene was realistic. He had watched the Democratic party, a bond of union between the two sections of the country, break apart in the year that was coming to an end. He had

1

*William H. Gist. As Governor of South Carolina, 1858–
1860, he called for secession in the event of Lincoln's election to the Presidency of the United States.*

seen a northern Union faction nominate the Illinoisan Stephen A.
Douglas. He had watched the more conservative Democrats, North
and South, gather to choose John C. Breckinridge of Kentucky. He
was aware that the Republican party, that put its first candidate
into the field four years earlier, was confident of victory. He knew
that the remnant of the Old Whigs, who called themselves the
Constitutional Union party and who had nominated John Bell of
Tennessee, would help make the election of Lincoln certain.

Gist's assessment was correct. On November 6 the voters of the
United States gave Lincoln 1,866,452 votes out of a total of 4,682,069.

2

His was a minority victory, but in the Electoral College he received 180 votes against 123 for his three opponents.

By that time Gist had received replies from most of the governors to whom he had sent his inquiry. Some equivocated but others were forthright. Governor A. B. Moore of Alabama wrote: "It is my opinion that Alabama will not secede alone, but if two or more States will cooperate with her, she will secede with them." John J. Pettus of Mississippi replied without reservation: "I will call our Legislature in extra session as soon as it is known that the Black Republicans have carried the election. I expect Mississippi will ask a council of the Southern States, and if that council advises secession Mississippi will go with them." The Governor of Georgia replied that in his opinion the people of Georgia, in the event of the election of Lincoln, would "meet all the Southern States in convention and take common action for the protection of the rights of all." "I . . . am proud to say that Florida," Governor M. S. Perry of that state answered, "is ready to wheel into line with the gallant Palmetto State, or any other Cotton State or States, in any course which she or they may in their judgment think proper to adopt. . . . If there is sufficient manliness in the South to strike for our rights, honor, and safety, in God's name let it be done before the inauguration of Lincoln."

The Cotton States line up behind South Carolina

South Carolina moved quickly to carry out Gist's promise. In mid-December, in response to a call of the Legislature, delegates to a convention assembled at Columbia. Finding the capital in the throes of a smallpox epidemic they adjourned to Charleston, but not before James L. Petigru, the only outspoken Unionist in the state, made a pointed quip. Asked by a visitor the location of the insane asylum, Petigru pointed to the Baptist Church where the convention was in session. "It looks like a church," he said, "but it is now a lunatic asylum: go there and you will find one hundred and sixty-four maniacs within."

To one sturdy South Carolinian, the Secessionists were insane

On December 18 the convention reassembled at Charleston. Crowds of excited people filled the streets and the stairways of the hall in which the delegates met. The streets were gay with bunting and flags and a holiday atmosphere pervaded the city. The convention took little time to report and pass by unanimous vote an ordinance of secession:

"We, the People of the State of South Carolina, in Convention assembled, do declare and ordain, and it is hereby declared and ordained,

"That the Ordinance adopted by us in Convention, on the twenty-third day of May, in the year of our Lord one thousand seven hundred and eighty-eight, whereby the Constitution of the United States of America was ratified, and also, all Acts and parts of Acts of the General Assembly of this State, ratifying amendments of the said Constitution, are hereby repealed; and that the union now subsisting between South

3

*John C. Breckinridge, candidate of
the conservative Democrats in 1860*

Carolina and other States, under the name of 'The United States of
America,' is hereby dissolved."

That evening in the presence of crowded galleries every member
of the convention signed the ordinance. At the conclusion of the
ceremony the audience broke into a storm of cheers, the ladies waved
their handkerchiefs, and the palmetto trees ornamenting the chamber
were torn to pieces for souvenirs. Outside, the city went wild with
excitement. Church bells pealed and cannon fired salutes. As one
observer commented: "The whole heart of the people had spoken."

*The basic cause of
disunion: Negro slavery*

What had brought this prosperous nation, the world's outstanding
example of democratic government, to disunion? Negro slavery? In
the end, yes, but it had taken almost two centuries for that blight to
become a serious divisive force. Throughout most of the colonial
period slavery prevailed in all the colonies although slaves were far
more numerous in those of the south than in those of the north. The
southern colonies had forced Thomas Jefferson to delete a paragraph
from the Declaration of Independence condemning George III for
condoning the slave trade, but the deletion had been accomplished
without excessive bitterness. Throughout the Revolution the southern
colonists had fought shoulder to shoulder with those of the north. The
presence of slavery had resulted in compromises in the Constitutional
Convention but had not prevented the adoption of the Constitution.

Early in the nineteenth century, however, the two sections of the
new nation began to move in different directions. In 1793 Eli Whitney,
a Yale graduate tutoring in Georgia, invented the cotton gin. The

4

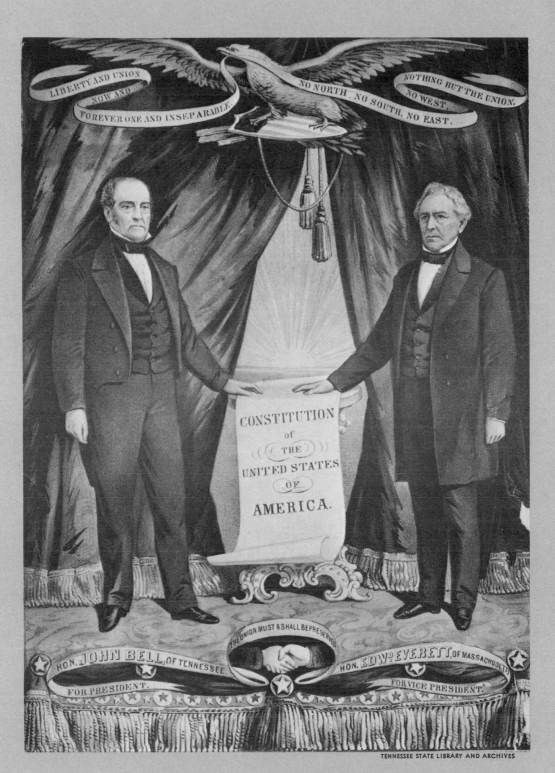

John Bell of Tennessee and Edward Everett of Massachu-setts, candidates of the Constitutional Union party in 1860

James L. Petigru, Charleston lawyer and Union-ist. To him, the entire state was a madhouse.

machine removed an inherent limit on the crop. As a result, production increased by leaps and bounds. The Negro, adapted to work in the cotton fields, became, in the eyes of southern planters, indispensable. Although the slave trade was prohibited after 1808, the number of slaves increased almost as rapidly as the number of bales of cotton that came from the plantations.

The North, however, began to outstrip the South in population and

South Bay Street in Charleston

wealth. According to the census of 1800 the United States contained 5,308,000 persons. Of this number, 2,622,000 lived in the states of the South. By 1850 the population had increased to 23,000,000. Of these, only 7,250,000 lived in the states that would secede. Ten years later, on the eve of war, the disparity between the two sections was even greater. Of a population of 31,000,000, more than 22,000,000 would cling to the Union with only 9,000,000 seceding. Of the cities with more than 100,000 inhabitants, six were located in the northern states. Two—St. Louis and Baltimore—stood in border states that would remain loyal. The deep South could claim only one, New Orleans.

The North pulls ahead of the South in population and wealth

Nor is population the only gauge of the difference between the two sections. The construction of railroads offers another measurement. In 1850, of the 8600 miles of railroad in the United States, the northern states possessed 6200 miles and the southern and border states 2400 miles. Ten years later the totals were 19,700 and 10,800.

In manufactures a similar disparity prevailed. To itemize the deficiencies of the South would be tedious. One Southerner summarized volumes of statistics when he declaimed in 1855:

7

Hall of the St. Andrew's Society in Charleston, where the Ordinance of Secession was adopted. Fire destroyed the building in 1861.

"From the rattle with which the nurse tickles the ear of the child born in the South to the shroud that covers the cold form of the dead, everything comes to us from the North. We rise from between sheets made in Northern looms, and pillows of Northern feathers, to wash in basins made in the North, dry our beards on Northern towels, and dress ourselves in garments woven in Northern looms; we eat from Northern plates and dishes; our rooms are swept with Northern brooms, our gardens dug with Northern spades, and our bread kneaded in trays or dishes of Northern wood or tin; and the very wood which feeds our fires is cut with Northern axes, helved with hickory brought from Connecticut or New York."

The South as poor relation

By the middle of the nineteenth century it was evident that economically the nation had split into two parts. Southern society rested on the production of cotton, tobacco, and other staple crops cultivated by slave labor. Northern society, agricultural, mechanical and commercial, was carried on by free labor. A clash between the two different systems was inevitable although its imminence was only imperfectly seen by men of the time.

The earliest overt conflict between North and South came in 1818 when Missouri sought admission to the Union with a constitution which permitted slavery. Her admission would upset the balance between free and slave states that had so far prevailed. Two years of bitter controversy resulted in the Missouri Compromise, which admitted the new state to the Union but provided that slavery would be excluded from much of the unorganized country lying to the west. The line of Missouri's southern boundary, 36°30′, was to be extended westward and the territory north of the line would be free soil.

Banner of the South Carolina Secession Convention. Of the states shown, Maryland, Kentucky, and Delaware remained loyal; Missouri, though divided, did not pass an ordinance of secession; Tennessee left the Union, declaring her independence.

CHARLESTON

MERCURY

EXTRA:

Passed unanimously at 1.15 o'clock, P. M., December 20th, 1860.

AN ORDINANCE

To dissolve the Union between the State of South Carolina and other States united with her under the compact entitled "The Constitution of the United States of America."

We, the People of the State of South Carolina, in Convention assembled, do declare and ordain, and it is hereby declared and ordained,

That the Ordinance adopted by us in Convention, on the twenty-third day of May, in the year of our Lord one thousand seven hundred and eighty-eight, whereby the Constitution of the United States of America was ratified, and also, all Acts and parts of Acts of the General Assembly of this State, ratifying amendments of the said Constitution, are hereby repealed; and that the union now subsisting between South Carolina and other States, under the name of "The United States of America," is hereby dissolved.

THE

UNION

IS

DISSOLVED!

This Charleston Mercury *was on the street a few minutes after the ordinance was adopted.*

The Compromise put an end temporarily to the controversy over slavery. The truce, however, was brief. On January 1, 1831, William Lloyd Garrison, confirmed abolitionist, published the first number of a militant anti-slavery periodical, *The Liberator*. Calling for an end to slavery he proclaimed, "I am in earnest—I will not equivocate—I will not excuse—I will not retreat a single inch—*and I will be heard*." With this publication Garrison touched off an abolitionist crusade

*The cotton gin:
Whitney's 1794 patent*

which put the South on the defensive. Abolitionist publications were barred from the mails south of the Mason-Dixon line and even the national House of Representatives adopted a "gag rule" which prevented the reception and discussion of anti-slavery petitions. The Mexican War, resulting in the acquisition of a vast area in the southwestern and western parts of the continent, intensified the differences between sections. Anti-slavery forces in Congress tried to stipulate through the Wilmot Proviso that slavery should be forever excluded from any territory acquired from Mexico. The South defeated the Proviso, but the controversy over it further inflamed sectional animosities.

In December, 1849, a long and bitter contest for Speaker of the House of Representatives brought tempers to the breaking point. For seventeen days Robert C. Winthrop of Massachusetts and Howell Cobb of Georgia were deadlocked. Southern radicals threatened secession; Northerners defied them. Many members of the House went armed and several hotheads flung challenges to duels. On the sixty-third ballot Cobb was chosen by a plurality. The contest, a step in

11

Slavery: the idyllic view. A painting of a cotton plantation by C. Giroux.

Slavery: the camera did not idealize.

Eli Whitney, as a young Yale graduate, invented the cotton gin while on a visit to Georgia in 1793.

the direction of disunity, had clarified issues. Extreme Southerners demanded that all the national territories should be open to slavery. Northerners wanted the territories kept free from slavery by congressional action. The South sought a more stringent fugitive slave law; the North, abolition of the slave trade in the District of Columbia.

When, in 1850, California applied for admission as a state and New Mexico and Utah for the formation of territorial governments, a crisis was precipitated. Henry Clay, ill and feeble, returned to the Senate to try to work out one of the compromises for which he was famous. Clay's measures, embodied in an omnibus bill, provided that California would come in as a free state, that New Mexico and Utah should be organized as territories without mention of slavery, that a much more stringent fugitive slave law be substituted for the one in force, and that

13

CREDIT SALE OF A CHOICE GANG OF 41
SLAVES!

COMPRISING MECHANICS, LABORERS, ETC,
FOR THE SETTLEMENT OF A CO-PARTNERSHIP OF RAILROAD CONTRACTORS·

BY J. A. BEARD & MAY, J. A. BEARD, AUCT'R.

WILL BE SOLD AT AUCTION, AT BANKS' ARCADE, MAGAZINE STREET,

ON TUESDAY, FEBRUARY 5th, 1856,
AT 12 O'CLOCK,
A VERY VALUABLE GANG OF SLAVES,

Belonging to a co-partnership, and sold to close the same. The said slaves comprise a gang of 41 choice Negroes. On the list will be found a good Blacksmith, one superior Bricklayer, Field Hands, Laborers, one Tanner, one Cooper, and a first rate woman Cook.

LEWIS, a black man, aged 32 good field hand and laborer.
SHELLY, do 26 do do
PHILIP, do 30 fair bricklayer.
HENRY, do 24 fair cooper.
JACOB BATES, do 22 good field hand and laborer.
BOB STAKELEY do 35 do do
COLUMBUS, do 21 do do
MARTIN, do 25 do do
GEORGE, do 30 No. 1 blacksmith.
WESTLY, a griff, 24 a fine tanner and bricklayer.
NELSON, a black man, 30 a good field hand and laborer.
DOCK, do 28 do do
BIG FRED, do 24 do do
LITTLE SOL, do 22 do do
ALFRED, a griff, 28 do do
SIMON, a black man, 21 do do
WATT, do 30 do do
JIM LEAVY, do 24 do do
JIM ALLEN, do 26 do do
FRANK GETTYS, a griff, 26 do do
JERRY GETTYS, a black, 23 do do
BILL GETTYS, do 23 do do
GRANDERSON, do 24 do do
LITTLE FED, do 23 do do
FRANK HENRY, a griff, 23 do do
EDMOND, do 21 do do
ANDERSON, a black man, 24 a No. 1 bricklayer and mason.
BOB SPRIGS, a griff, 25 a good field hand and laborer.
ELIJAH, a black man, 35 do do
JACK, do 30 do do
REUBEN, do 28 unsound.
STEPHEN, do 22 a good field hand and laborer.
YELLOW JERRY, a griff, 28 a good teamster.
BIG SOL, a black man, 26 a good field hand and laborer.
BILL COLLINS, do 28 do do
JESS, do 26 do do
JUDGE, do 30 do do
JERRY CARTER, do 28 do do

LOUISA, a griff, 38 years, a good Cook and seamstress, and an excellent servant.
ROBERT, 13 years old, defect in one toe.
JASPAR, 24 years old, an extra No. 1 laborer, driver and coachman.
The slaves can be seen four days previous to the day of sale. They are fully guarantied against the vices and maladies prescribed by law, and are all selected slaves.

TERMS OF SALE—One year's credit for approved city acceptances or endorsed paper, with interest at 7 per cent. from date, and mortgage on the slaves if required
ACTS OF SALE BEFORE WM. SHANNON, NOTARY PUBLIC, AT THE EXPENSE OF THE PURCHASERS.

After the sale of the above list of Slaves, will be sold Another lot of Negroes, comprising Field Hands, House servants and Mechanics. A full description of the same will be given at the sale. The slaves can be seen two days previous to the sale.

Slavery in grimmest realism. Prices ranged from $750 for Reuben, "unsound," to $2700 for Anderson, "a No. 1 bricklayer and mason."

THE LIBERATOR.

VOL. I.] WILLIAM LLOYD GARRISON AND ISAAC KNAPP, PUBLISHERS. **[NO. 1.**

BOSTON, MASSACHUSETTS.] OUR COUNTRY IS THE WORLD—OUR COUNTRYMEN ARE MANKIND. [SATURDAY, JANUARY 1, 1831.

THE LIBERATOR
IS PUBLISHED WEEKLY
AT NO. 6, MERCHANTS' HALL.

WM. L. GARRISON, EDITOR.

Stephen Foster, Printer.

TERMS.

☞ Two Dollars per annum, payable in advance.

☞ Agents allowed every sixth copy gratis.

☞ No subscription will be received for a shorter period than six months.

☞ All letters and communications must be POST PAID.

THE LIBERATOR.

THE SALUTATION.

To date my being from the opening year,
I come, a stranger in this busy sphere,
Where some I meet perchance may pause and ask,
What is my name, my purpose, or my task?

My name is 'LIBERATOR'! I propose
To hurl my shafts at freedom's deadliest foes!
My task is hard—for I am charged to save
Man from his brother!—to redeem the slave!

Ye who may hear, and yet condemn my cause,
Say, shall the best of Nature's holy laws
Be trodden down? and shall her open veins
Flow but for cement to her offspring's chains?

Art thou a parent? shall thy children be
Rent from thy breast, like branches from the tree,
And doom'd to servitude, in helplessness,
On other shores, and thou ask no redress?

Thou, in whose bosom glows the sacred flame
Of filial love, say, if the tyrant came,
To force thy parent shrieking from thy sight,
Would thy heart bleed—*because thy face is white?*

Art thou a brother? shall thy sister twine
Her feeble arm in agony on thine,
And thou not lift the heel, nor aim the blow
At him who bears her off to life-long wo?

Art thou a sister? will no desp'rate cry
Awake thy sleeping brother, while thine eye
Beholds the fetters locking on the limb
Stretched out in rest, which hence, must end, for him?

Art thou a lover?---no! naught e'er was found
In lover's breast, save cords of love, that bound
Man to his kind! then, thy professions save!
Forswear affection, or release thy slave!

Thou who art kneeling at thy Maker's shrine,
Ask if Heaven takes such offerings as thine!
If in thy bonds the son of Afric sighs,
Far higher than thy prayer his groan will rise!

God is a God of mercy, and would see
The prison-doors unbarr'd---the bondmen free!
He is a God of truth, with purer eyes
Than to behold the oppressor's sacrifice!

Avarice, thy cry and thine insatiate thirst
Make man consent to see his brother cursed!
Tears, sweat and blood thou drink'st, but in their turn,
They shall cry 'more!' while vengeance bids thee burn.

The Lord hath said it!---who shall him gainsay?
He says, 'the wicked, they shall go away'——
Who are the wicked?——Contradict who can,
They are the oppressors of their fellow man!

Aid me, NEW ENGLAND! 'tis my hope in you
Which gives me strength my purpose to pursue!
Do you not hear your sister States resound
With Afric's cries to have her sons unbound?

* * *

TO THE PUBLIC.

In the month of August, I issued proposals for publishing 'THE LIBERATOR,' in Washington city; but the enterprise, though hailed in different sections of the country, was palsied by public indifference. Since that time, the removal of the Genius of Universal Emancipation to the Seat of Government has rendered less imperious the establishment of a similar periodical in that quarter.

During my recent tour for the purpose of exciting the minds of the people by a series of discourses on the subject of slavery, every place that I visited gave fresh evidence of the fact, that a greater revolution in public sentiment was to be effected in the free states—*and particularly in New-England*—than at the south. I found contempt more bitter, opposition more active, detraction more relentless, prejudice more stubborn, and apathy more frozen, than among slave owners themselves. Of course, there were individual exceptions to the contrary. This state of things afflicted, but did not dishearten me. I determined, at every hazard, to lift up the standard of emancipation in the eyes of the nation, *within sight of Bunker Hill and in the birth place of liberty.* That standard is now unfurled; and long may it float, unhurt by the spoliations of time or the missiles of a desperate foe—yea, till every chain be broken, and every bondman set free! Let southern oppressors tremble—let their secret abettors tremble—let their northern apologists tremble—let all the enemies of the persecuted blacks tremble.

I deem the publication of my original Prospectus * unnecessary, as it has obtained a wide circulation. The principles therein inculcated will be steadily pursued in this paper, excepting that I shall not array myself as the political partisan of any man. In defending the great cause of human rights, I wish to derive the assistance of all religions and of all parties.

Assenting to the 'self-evident truth' maintained in the American Declaration of Independence, 'that all men are created equal, and endowed by their Creator with certain inalienable rights—among which are life, liberty and the pursuit of happiness,' I shall strenuously contend for the immediate enfranchisement of our slave population. In Park-street Church, on the Fourth of July, 1829, in an address on slavery, I unreflectingly assented to the popular but pernicious doctrine of *gradual* abolition. I seize this opportunity to make a full and unequivocal recantation, and thus publicly to ask pardon of my God, of my country, and of my brethren the poor slaves, for having uttered a sentiment so full of timidity, injustice and absurdity. A similar recantation, from my pen, was published in the Genius of Universal Emancipation at Baltimore, in September, 1829. My conscience is now satisfied.

I am aware, that many object to the severity of my language; but is there not cause for severity? I *will be* as harsh as truth, and as uncompromising as justice. On this subject, I do not wish to think, or speak, or write, with moderation. No! no! Tell a man whose house is on fire, to give a moderate alarm; tell him to moderately rescue his wife from the hands of the ravisher; tell the mother to gradually extricate her babe from the fire into which it has fallen;—but urge me not to use moderation in a cause like the present. I am in earnest—I will not equivocate—I will not excuse—I will not retreat a single inch—AND I WILL BE HEARD. The apathy of the people is enough to make every statue leap from its pedestal, and to hasten the resurrection of the dead.

It is pretended, that I am retarding the cause of emancipation by the coarseness of my invective, and the precipitancy of my measures. *The charge is not true.* On this question my influence,---humble as it is,---is felt at this moment to a considerable extent, and shall be felt in coming years---not perniciously, but beneficially—not as a curse, but as a blessing; and posterity will bear testimony that I was right. I desire to thank God, that he enables me to disregard 'the fear of man which bringeth a snare,' and to speak his truth in its simplicity and power. And here I close with this fresh dedication:

'Oppression! I have seen thee, face to face,
And met thy cruel eye and cloudy brow;
But thy soul-withering glance I fear not now—
For dread to prouder feelings doth give place
Of deep abhorrence! Scorning the disgrace
Of slavish knees that at thy footstool bow,
I also kneel—but with far other vow
Do hail thee and thy herd of hirelings base:—
I swear, while life-blood warms my throbbing veins,
Still to oppose and thwart, with heart and hand,
Thy brutalising sway—till Afric's chains
Are burst, and Freedom rules the rescued land,—
Trampling Oppression and his iron rod:
Such is the vow I take—SO HELP ME GOD!'

WILLIAM LLOYD GARRISON.

BOSTON, January 1, 1831.

*I would here offer my grateful acknowledgments to those editors who so promptly and generously inserted my Proposals. They must give me an available opportunity to repay their liberality.

DISTRICT OF COLUMBIA.

What do many of the professed enemies of slavery mean, by heaping all their reproaches upon the south, and asserting that the crime of oppression is not national? What power but Congress—and Congress by the authority of the American people—has jurisdiction over the District of Columbia? That District is rotten with the plague, and stinks in the nostrils of the world. Though it is the Seat of our National Government,—open to the daily inspection of foreign ambassadors,—and ostensibly opulent with the congregated wisdom, virtue and intelligence of the land,—yet a fouler spot scarcely exists on earth. In it the worst features of slavery are exhibited; and as a mart for slave traders, it is unequalled. These facts are well known to our two or three hundred representatives, but no remedy is proposed; they are known, if not minutely at least generally, to our whole population,—but who calls for redress?

Hitherto, a few straggling petitions, relative to this subject, have gone into Congress; but they have been too few to denote much public anxiety, or to command a deferential notice. It is certainly time that a vigorous and systematic effort should be made, from one end of the country to the other, to pull down that national monument of oppression which towers up in the District. We do hope that the 'earthquake voice' of the people will this session shake the black fabric to its foundation.

The following petition is now circulating in this city, and has obtained several valuable signatures. A copy may be found at the Bookstore of LINCOLN & EDMANDS, No. 59, Washington-street, for a few days longer, where all the friends of the cause are earnestly invited to go and subscribe.

Petition to Congress for the Abolition of Slavery in the District of Columbia.

To the Honorable Senate and House of Representatives of the United States of America in Congress assembled, the petition of the undersigned citizens of Boston in Massachusetts and its vicinity respectfully represents—

That your petitioners are deeply impressed with the evils arising from the existence of slavery in the District of Columbia. While our Declaration of Independence boldly proclaims as self-evident truths, 'that all men are created equal, that they are endowed by their Creator with certain inalienable rights, that among these are life, liberty, and the pursuit of happiness,'—at the very seat of government human beings are born, almost daily, whom the laws pronounce to be from their birth, not *equal* to other men, and who are, for life, deprived of *liberty* and the free *pursuit of happiness.* The inconsistency of the conduct of our nation with its political creed, has brought down upon it the just and severe reprehension of foreign nations.

In addition to the other evils flowing from slavery, both moral and political, which it is needless to specify, circumstances have rendered this District a common resort for traders in human flesh, who bring into it their captives in chains, and lodge them in places of confinement, previously to their being carried to the markets of the south and west.

From the small number of slaves in the District of Columbia, and the moderate proportion which they bear to the free population there, the difficulties, which in most of the slaveholding states oppose the restoration of this degraded class of men to their natural rights, do not exist.

Your petitioners therefore pray that Congress will, without delay, take such measures for the immediate or gradual abolition of Slavery in the District of Columbia, and for preventing the bringing of slaves into that District for purposes of traffic, in such mode, as may be thought advisable; and that suitable provision be made for the education of all free blacks and colored children in the District, thus to preserve them from continuing, even as free men, an unenlightened and degraded caste.

If any individual should be unmoved, either by the petition or the introductory remarks, the following article will startle his apathy, unless he be morally dead—dead—dead. Read it—read it! The language of the editor is remarkable for its energy, considering the quarter whence it emanates. After all, we are not the only fanatics in the land!

[From the Washington Spectator, of Dec. 4.]

THE SLAVE TRADE IN THE CAPITAL.

'The tender ties of father, husband, friend,
All bonds of nature in that moment end,
And each endures, while yet he draws his breath,
A stroke as fatal as the scythe of death;
They lose in tears, the far receding shore,
But not the thought that they must meet no more!'

It is well, perhaps, the American people should know, that while we reiterate our boasts of liberty in the ears of the nations, and send back across the Atlantic our shouts of joy at the triumph of liberty in France, we ourselves are busily engaged in the work of oppression. Yes, let it be known to the citizens of America, that at the very time when the procession which contained the President of the United States and his Cabinet was marching in triumph to the Capitol, to celebrate the victory of the French people over their oppressors, another kind of procession was marching another way, and that consisted of colored human beings, handcuffed in pairs, and driven along by what had the appearance of a man on a horse! A similar scene was repeated on Saturday last; a *drove* consisting of males and females chained in couples, starting from Roby's tavern on foot, for Alexandria, where, with others, they are to embark on board a slave-ship in waiting to convey them to the South. While we are writing, a colored man enters our room, and begs us to inform him if we can point out any person who will redeem his friend now immured in Alexandria jail, in a state of distress amounting almost to distraction.* He has been a faithful servant of a revolutionary officer who recently died—has been sold at auction—parted from affectionate parents—and from decent and mourning friends. Our own servant, with others, of whom we can speak in commendatory terms, went down to Alexandria to bid him farewell, but they were refused admission to his cell, as was said, 'the sight of his friends made him feel so.' He bears the reputation of a pious man. It is but a few weeks since we saw a ship with her cargo of slaves in the port of Norfolk, Va.; on passing up the river, saw another ship off Alexandria, swarming with the victims of human cupidity. Such are the scenes enacting in the heart of the American nation. Oh patriotism! where is thy indignation? Oh philanthropy! where is thy grief? OH SHAME, WHERE IS THY BLUSH? Well may the generous and noble minded O'Connell say of the American citizen, '*I tell him he is a hypocrite. Look at the stain in your star-spangled standard that was never struck down in battle. I turn from the Declaration of American Independence, and I tell him that he has declared to God and man a lie, and before God and man I arraign him as a hypocrite.*' Yes, thou soul of fire, glorious O'Connell, if thou could but witness the spectacles in Washington that make the genius of liberty droop her head in shame, and weep her tears away in deep silence and undissembled sorrow, you would lift your voice even to tones of thunder, but you would make yourself heard. Where is the O'Connell of this republic that will plead for the EMANCIPATION OF THE DISTRICT OF COLUMBIA? These shocking scenes must cease from amongst us, or we must cease to call ourselves free; ay, and we must cease to expect the mercy of God—we must prepare for the coming judgment of Him who, as our charter acknowledges, made all men '*free and equal!*'

* At the same time this man was sold, another—a husband—was knocked off. The tears and agonies of his wife made such an impression on the mind of a generous spectator that he bought him back.

When a premium of Fifty Dollars is offered for the best theatrical poem, our newspapers advertise the fact with great unanimity. The following is incomparably more important.

PREMIUM.

A Premium of Fifty Dollars, the Donation of a benevolent individual in the State of Maine, and now deposited with the Treasurer of the Pennsylvania Society for promoting the Abolition of Slavery, &c. is offered to the author of the best Treatise on the following subject: 'The Duties of Ministers and Churches of all denominations to avoid the stain of Slavery, and to make the holding of Slaves a barrier to communion and church membership.'

The composition to be directed (post paid) to either of the subscribers—the name of the author in a separate sealed paper, which will be destroyed if his work shall be rejected.

Six months from this date are allowed for the purpose of receiving the Essays.

The publication and circulation of the preferred Tract will be regulated by the Pennsylvania Society above mentioned.

W. RAWLE,
J. PRESTON,
THOMAS SHIPLEY, } *Committee.*

Philadelphia, Oct. 11.

Page one of The Liberator, *Vol. I, No. 1. Garrison's famous pledge may be found in the fourth paragraph of the second column.*

William Lloyd Garrison, founder and editor of The Liberator

Henry Clay. In his last term as Senator from Kentucky he framed the Compromise of 1850.

Daniel Webster. His support of the Compromise of 1850 aroused the anger of many of his constituents in Massachusetts.

Dred Scott. In denying him freedom and citizenship the Supreme Court gave impetus to the newly formed Republican party.

the slave trade should be abolished in the District of Columbia. In support of these proposals Clay made his last great speech, begging extremists to abandon a course leading to disunion. John C. Calhoun, too near death to read his speech, deplored the growth of abolitionism and pleaded that the causes of Southern discontent must be removed if the Union were to be saved. Daniel Webster, also nearing the end of his life, braved the wrath of his New England constituents and supported Clay's measures. Due largely to the tactical skill of Senator Stephen A. Douglas of Illinois the measures were adopted. Moderates, a majority in both sections, believed that the Compromise of 1850 would settle the slavery question, if not permanently at least for many years.

The settlement turned out to be short-lived. In 1854 Douglas, chairman of the Committee on Territories, introduced a bill to organize the territories of Kansas and Nebraska. His motives were mixed, but high among them was a desire that the projected transcontinental railroad should follow a central route rather than a southern one. Douglas found that the South, in return for its support, would demand that his bill include a provision repealing the Missouri Compromise of 1820. Indifferent to slavery, he acceded, and the bill was amended to provide that the inhabitants of the territories themselves should decide whether or not they wanted to legalize slavery. Under heavy pressure from the administration of Franklin Pierce, the bill passed.

Roger B. Taney, Chief Justice of the United States, 1835–1864. Although his was only one of seven majority opinions in the Dred Scott case, it was generally accepted as the verdict of the court. On March 4, 1861, Taney would administer the oath of office to Lincoln.

In angry protest against the repeal of the Missouri Compromise, the Republican party is born

The result was an almost instant political explosion in the North. Abraham Lincoln, long a member of the Whig party, described his own revulsion at this turnabout in national policy. "In 1854," he said (writing of himself in the third person), "his profession had almost superseded the thought of politics in his mind, when the repeal of the Missouri Compromise aroused him as he had never been before." Protest meetings took place in dozens of towns and cities throughout the North. One such meeting in Ripon, Wisconsin, became the seed of the Republican party. In the beginning the party attracted few but abolitionists, but by 1856 it had drawn a sufficient following to put its own presidential candidate, John C. Frémont, into the field and to poll 1,341,000 votes out of a total of 4,054,000. In that same year Lincoln became a member of the party and was soon looked upon as its leader in Illinois.

In 1857 the Supreme Court of the United States contributed to the mounting tension by its decision in the case of Dred Scott. Scott, a Negro slave, had been taken by his master from St. Louis, Missouri, to Illinois and later to Wisconsin Territory, where slavery was prohibited.

After several years he was returned to St. Louis. Scott sued for his freedom in the Missouri courts on the ground that he had become a free man because of his residence in a free state and a free territory. The judgment in Scott's favor was overruled in the State Supreme Court. The case was appealed to the Federal courts and eventually to the United States Supreme Court. In separate opinions a majority of the justices decided against Scott on the ground that a Negro slave was not a citizen of the United States or the state of Missouri and therefore could not sue in a Federal court. The justices proceeded to complicate the situation by holding the Missouri Compromise unconstitutional. Northerners denounced the decision as a conspiracy and the political atmosphere became more ominous than ever.

The Dred Scott decision intensifies sectional discord

In 1858 the senatorial term of Stephen A. Douglas came to an end. By common consent Abraham Lincoln opposed him. Lincoln began his campaign with a sensational speech.

"Mr. President and Gentlemen of the Convention," he said at Springfield on June 16, "if we could first know *where* we are, and *whither* we are tending, we could then better judge *what* to do, and *how* to do it.

"We are now far into the *fifth* year, since a policy was initiated, with

The Illinois State House, Springfield. In this building Lincoln delivered his "House Divided" speech. As President-elect, he occupied the Governor's office for several months in 1860.

Brevet Colonel
Robert E. Lee, U.S.A.,
as superintendent of
the United States Military
Academy, 1852–1855

the *avowed* object, and *confident* promise, of putting an end to slavery agitation.

"Under the operation of that policy, that agitation has not only, *not ceased,* but has *constantly augmented.*

The Union, Lincoln asserts, must cease to be divided between slavery and freedom

"In *my* opinion, it *will* not cease, until a *crisis* shall have been reached, and passed.

" 'A house divided against itself cannot stand.'

"I believe this government cannot endure, permanently half *slave* and half *free.*

"I do not expect the Union to be *dissolved*—I do not expect the house to *fall*—but I *do* expect it will cease to be divided.

"It will become *all* one thing, or *all* the other.

"Either the *opponents* of slavery, will arrest the further spread of it, and place it where the public mind shall rest in the belief that it is in

20

course of ultimate extinction; or its *advocates* will push it forward, till it shall become alike lawful in *all* the states, *old* as well as *new—North* as well as *South*."

Douglas plunged into his campaign with his customary aggressiveness. Early in July he addressed a huge meeting of his followers in Chicago; Lincoln replied to him the following day. A week later Douglas spoke in Springfield; Lincoln answered that evening. On July 24 Lincoln challenged Douglas to a series of joint debates. With some reluctance Douglas accepted.

Seven debates were scheduled, each to be held in one of the state's congressional districts where neither candidate had yet spoken. Each debate was to consist of a one-hour opening statement, a reply of an hour and a half, and a thirty-minute rejoinder. The first debate took place at Ottawa, Illinois, on August 21, the last at Alton on October 15. Throughout this period, and for two weeks before and afterward, both candidates addressed their own party rallies almost daily.

The debates attracted nationwide attention. They were stenographically reported, published in full in some newspapers, summarized in many others. They clarified not only for those who heard them but for thoughtful people everywhere the essence of the slavery question. Lincoln argued that slavery was "a moral, a social, and a political wrong" and that it was the duty of the Federal government to prohibit its extension into the territories. Douglas, on the other hand, proposed the doctrine of "popular sovereignty," by which the inhabitants of the territories themselves would decide whether or not they wanted slavery. To the moral issue he was completely indifferent, stating that he did not care whether slavery was voted up or down. Far transcending slavery in importance, as he saw it, was the fundamental principle of self-government.

Douglas won re-election. In 1858 senators were elected by the state legislatures and the apportionment of the Legislature of Illinois did not reflect accurately recent changes in population. The popular vote for Illinois state officers told a different story. The Republicans polled 125,430 votes for their state ticket, the Douglas Democrats 121,609, and the Buchanan Democrats 5071. The result demonstrated to the South that the Republican party was steadily growing in strength and that its determined opposition to the spread of slavery was almost certain to be successful. The campaign also proved that for the Southern extremists Douglas was an uncertain ally. He had admitted that he was indifferent to slavery; the fire-eaters of the South wanted an ardent proponent. As for Lincoln, what appeared to be a defeat was in fact an advantage. In three months he graduated from a local politician known only in his own state to a Republican leader with a national reputation.

Lincoln loses to Douglas in the senatorial campaign of 1858 but wins a national reputation

21

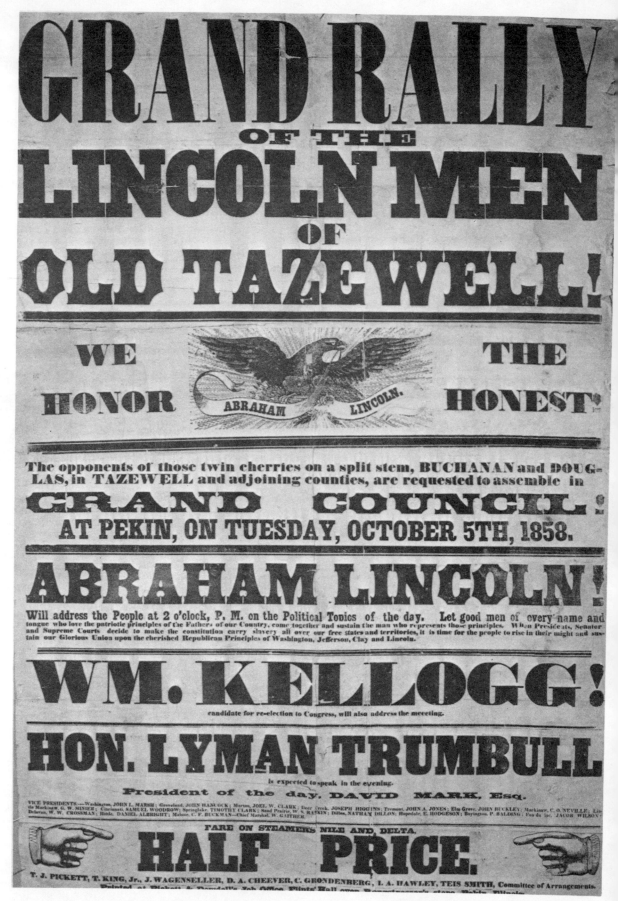

GRAND RALLY

OF THE

LINCOLN MEN

OF

OLD TAZEWELL!

WE   ABRAHAM   LINCOLN.   **THE**

HONOR   **HONEST**

The opponents of those twin cherries on a split stem, BUCHANAN and DOUG-
LAS, in TAZEWELL and adjoining counties, are requested to assemble in

GRAND COUNCIL!

AT PEKIN, ON TUESDAY, OCTOBER 5TH, 1858.

ABRAHAM LINCOLN!

Will address the People at 2 o'clock, P. M. on the Political Topics of the day. Let good men of every name and
tongue who love the patriotic principles of the Fathers of our Country, come together and sustain the man who represents those principles. When Presidents, Senator
and Supreme Courts decide to make the constitution carry slavery all over our free states and territories, it is time for the people to rise in their might and sustain our Glorious Union upon the cherished Republican Principles of Washington, Jefferson, Clay and Lincoln.

WM. KELLOGG!

candidate for re-election to Congress, will also address the meeting.

HON. LYMAN TRUMBULL

is expected to speak in the evening.

President of the day. DAVID MARK, Esq.

VICE PRESIDENTS—Washington, JOHN L. MARSH; Groveland, JOHN HANCOCK; Morton, JOEL W. CLARK; Deer Creek, JOSEPH HIGGINS; Tremont, JOHN A. JONES; Elm Grove, JOHN BUCKLEY; Mackinaw, C. O. NEVILLE; Little Mackinaw, G. W. MINIER; Cincinnati, SAMUEL WOODROW; Springlake, TIMOTHY CLARK; Sand Prairie, W. S. RANKIN; Dillon, NATHAN DILLON; Hopedale, E. HODGESON; Boynton, P. BALDING; Fon du lac, JACOB WILSON;
Delavan, W. W. CROSSMAN; Hittle, DANIEL ALBRIGHT; Malone, C. F. BUCKMAN—Chief Marshal, W. GAITHER.

FARE ON STEAMERS NILE AND DELTA.

HALF PRICE.

T. J. PICKETT, T. KING, Jr., J. WAGENSELLER, D. A. CHEEVER, C. GRONDENBERG, I. A. HAWLEY, TEIS SMITH, Committee of Arrangements.
Printed at Pickett & Derudell's Job Office, Flints' Hall over Bennetnesser's store, Pekin, Illinois.

A poster announcing a Republican meeting in the course of the Lincoln-Douglas debates. As far as is known, this is the only poster of the campaign that has been preserved.

Stephen A. Douglas, U.S. Senator from Illinois, 1847–1861. He defeated Lincoln for Senator in 1858, and was his principal opponent in the presidential campaign of 1860.

A year and a day after the last Lincoln-Douglas debate an antislavery fanatic, John Brown, put in motion a plot which he hoped would lead to a general slave revolt. On October 16, 1859, Brown and his band of thirteen whites and five Negroes seized the United States Arsenal at Harpers Ferry, Virginia. Two days later, after a short fight, the survivors were captured by a military force headed by Colonel Robert E. Lee, a Regular Army officer who happened to be in Washington when the troops were mustered. Accompanying Lee as his aide was Lieutenant J. E. B. Stuart, also of the Regular Army. Brown was charged with treason against the state of Virginia, given a fair trial, sentenced to death, and executed on December 2, 1859. His harebrained scheme made Southerners increasingly apprehensive of slave uprisings, while to the radical abolitionists he became a martyr. In less than two years, thousands of Northern boys would march to the refrain, "John Brown's Body Lies a-Mould'ring in the Grave."

Thoughtful people throughout the United States, aware of the mounting tensions, realized that the presidential election of 1860 would be of critical importance. The Democratic National Convention assembled at Charleston, South Carolina, on April 23. Douglas, the leading candidate for the nomination, immediately encountered the determined

PRUCLAMATIUN!

IN pursuance of instructions from the Governor of Virginia, notice is hereby given to all whom it may concern,

That, as heretofore, particularly from now until after Friday next the 2nd of December, STRANGERS found within the County of Jefferson, and Counties adjacent, having no known and proper business here, and who cannot give a satisfactory account of themselves, will be at once arrested.

That on, and for a proper period before that day, stangers and especially parties, approaching under the pretext of being present at the execution of John Brown, whether by Railroad or otherwise, will be met by the Military and turned back or arrested without regard to the amount of force, that may be required to affect this, and during the said period and especially on the 2nd of December, the citizens of Jefferson and the surrounding country are *EMPHATICALLY* warned to remain at their homes armed and guard their own property,

Information received from reliable sources, clearly indicates that by so doing they will best consult their own interests.

No WOMEN or CHILDREN will be allowed to come near the place of execution.

WM. B. TALLIAFERRO, *Maj. Gen. Com. troops,*
S. BASSETT FRENCH, *Military Sec'y.*
THOMAS C. GREEN, *Mayor,*
ANDREW HUNTER, *Asst. Pros. Att'y.*
JAMES W. CAMPBELL, *Sheriff.*

November 26th, '59.   Spirit Print.

A warning by the Governor of Virginia: no strangers will be allowed to witness the execution of John Brown.

John Brown, anti-slavery fanatic

COURTESY OF VICTOR D. SPARK

Brown on his way to the scaffold. A drawing by A. Berghaus.

opposition of the party's Southern extremists. In fifty-seven ballots he could not obtain the necessary two-thirds majority. Recognizing the hopelessness of the situation, the Convention adjourned to meet in Baltimore two months later. There on June 23 a similar deadlock was broken by the withdrawal of the Southern delegates. Douglas was nominated on the second ballot. The bolters organized a convention of their own and nominated the Kentuckian, John C. Breckinridge, as their candidate.

Before this time, in mid-May, the Republican National Convention had met in Chicago. The delegates had been expected to nominate William H. Seward of New York, the acknowledged leader of the party. Failing Seward, Salmon P. Chase of Ohio appeared to be the most likely choice. After the Convention met, it became apparent that both Seward and Chase, who had long been in public life, had acquired many powerful enemies. Delegates from states essential to victory asserted heatedly that with either Seward or Chase at the head of the ticket they could not succeed. Eyes turned to Abraham Lincoln, who enjoyed the endorsement of only his own state. He had not been before the public long enough to acquire the enemies who were blocking the nomination of Seward and Chase. He came from a pivotal state, he enjoyed the national notice which the debates with Douglas had given

Abraham Lincoln, dark horse, wins the Republican nomination

25

Abraham Lincoln, President-elect, 1860

Salmon P. Chase of Ohio, the favorite of the radical wing of the Republican party for the presidential nomination in 1860

William Henry Seward of New York, Lincoln's principal rival for the Republican nomination in 1860

him, and he possessed the log cabin birth and boyhood of frontier hardship that at that time appealed so strongly to the American people. On the third ballot he won the nomination. The split in the Democratic party and the candidacy of John Bell of Tennessee, on the Constitutional Union ticket, virtually guaranteed Lincoln's election, bringing on the crisis which Governor Gist of South Carolina had foreseen.

Lincoln, in his modest office in Springfield, Illinois, refused to panic at the news of South Carolina's secession. He said nothing publicly but he did indicate to friends that he would not allow the Union to fall apart without making every effort to hold it together. To Elihu B. Washburne in Congress he wrote on December 21: "Last night I received your letter giving an account of your interview with Gen. Scott, and for which I thank you. Please present my respects to the General, and tell him, confidentially, I shall be obliged to him to be as well prepared as he can to either *hold,* or *retake,* the forts, *as* the case may require, at, and after the inauguration." Similar letters went to other confidants in the capital.

The President-elect will not permit the South to secede in peace

NEW YORK HISTORICAL SOCIETY

Fort Sumter, Charleston Harbor, 1860

Major Robert Anderson of Kentucky, loyal to the Union, garrisons Fort Sumter

In the last days of 1860 the majority of the people of the North refused to believe that the Union stood on the edge of dissolution. The South had threatened to secede so often that most Northerners considered this to be only another bluff with no more substance than those which had preceded it. However, South Carolina gave every evidence of sincerity and determination. Private military companies paraded and drilled. By the end of the year they had guns trained on Fort Moultrie in Charleston Harbor. For five weeks the fort had been commanded by Major Robert Anderson, a popular Kentuckian. Anderson, though sympathizing with the South, was a loyal officer determined to carry out his responsibilities as best he could. Knowing that Moultrie was vulnerable from the land side, he decided to transfer his garrison to Fort Sumter, a much stronger fortification, but then unfinished. On the night of December 26 he made the move in the utmost secrecy. When day broke, the Union flag over Sumter infuriated the people of Charleston.

1861

WAR COMES

I N THE FIRST MONTH of the new year other Southern states followed the lead of South Carolina. Mississippi, by an ordinance of secession, declared herself out of the Union on January 9; Florida on January 10; Alabama on January 11; Georgia on January 19; Louisiana on January 26; and Texas on February 1. On February 4 delegates from all these states except Texas met at Montgomery, Alabama, to form a provisional government for the Confederate States of America. There they adopted a provisional constitution modeled on that of the United States. The provisional Congress proceeded to issue $1,000,000 in treasury notes and provided for raising 100,000 volunteers to serve twelve months. It passed acts to organize a navy, post office, and courts, and authorized the sending of commissioners to Europe to make treaties of friendship and commerce. The states turned over to the Confederacy the property of the national government which they had seized, and Louisiana received a special vote of thanks for giving up $536,000 in coin which she had confiscated from the mint and customhouse in New Orleans.

On February 9 the provisional Confederate Congress chose Jefferson Davis President and Alexander H. Stephens Vice President to serve until February 22, 1862, when the permanent government would go into effect. Davis, a fifty-three-year-old Mississippian, was a West

Jefferson Davis of Mississippi, inaugurated as Provisional President of the Confederate States of America on February 18, 1861

Alexander H. Stephens of Georgia, Provisional Vice President of the Confederacy

SOUTH CAROLINA

Point graduate who had served in the Black Hawk and Mexican wars. He had been Secretary of War in Pierce's cabinet and had served most of two terms in the United States Senate, resigning upon the secession of Mississippi. Stephens, a Georgian, had been in Congress for eight terms, including the one in which Lincoln had been a representative from Illinois. The two men had become friendly enough for Lincoln, two days after South Carolina's secession, to appeal to the Georgian for understanding. "Do the people of the South really entertain fears that a Republican administration would, *directly,* or *indirectly* interfere with their slaves or with them, about their slaves? If they do, I wish to assure you, as once a friend, and still, I hope, not an enemy, that there is no cause for such fears."

From Springfield, Lincoln sent counsel to Republicans in Washington, where efforts to compromise the differences between the two sections were being made. To Senator William H. Seward, whom he had already chosen to be his Secretary of State, he wrote:

"I say now . . . as I have all the while said, that on the territorial question—that is, the question of extending slavery under the national auspices,—I am inflexible. I am for no compromise which *assists* or *permits* the extension of the institution on soil owned by the nation. And any trick by which the nation is to acquire territory, and then allow some local authority to spread slavery over it, is as obnoxious as any other."

Lincoln had already been at work on his inaugural address. Taking with him only Henry Clay's speech in support of the Compromise of 1850, Andrew Jackson's proclamation against nullification, and a copy of the Constitution, he retired each day to a vacant second-story room facing the State House. With a printed copy of the address in his carpetbag he left Springfield on February 11 for a trip to Washington that would take almost two weeks. On the way he spoke frequently, but only on one or two occasions did he say anything of consequence regarding the national crisis. The sharpest of these comments came when he addressed the General Assembly of New Jersey at Trenton. "I shall do all that may be in my power," he said, "to promote a peaceful settlement of all our difficulties. The man does not live who is more devoted to peace than I am. None who would do more to preserve it. But it may be necessary to put the foot down firmly." At this point the audience broke into cheers so loud and long that Lincoln could not continue for several minutes. "And if I do my duty," he concluded,

CHICAGO HISTORICAL SOCIETY

The inauguration of Davis and Stephens at Montgomery, Alabama, February 18, 1861

"and do right, you will sustain me, will you not?" Another storm of cheers answered his question.

Though the sun shone March 4, 1861, when the new President took office, the day was raw and disagreeable.

In spite of the sharp winds, thousands of people lined Pennsylvania Avenue as Lincoln and retiring President Buchanan drove from the White House to the Capitol in a barouche drawn by four white horses. Soldiers and District of Columbia militia lined the street and sharpshooters lay on roofs behind parapets ready in case of an attempt at assassination. After watching the induction of Hannibal Hamlin, Vice President, in the Senate Chamber, Lincoln was escorted to the outdoor platform at the east portico of the Capitol, where 10,000 curious spectators had gathered. Chief Justice Taney administered the oath of office and the new President spoke his inaugural address.

Standing in the sights of sharpshooters' rifles, Lincoln takes the oath of office

His tone was pacific, but a vein of iron ran through his words. The accession of a Republican administration, he told the people of the Southern states, did not threaten their property, their peace, their personal security. Beyond a doubt, the Constitution contemplated a perpetual union. No state of its own motion could lawfully secede. To the extent of his ability he would execute the laws throughout the nation. "In doing this," he asserted, "there needs to be no bloodshed or violence; and there shall be none, unless it be forced upon the national authority. The power confided to me, will be used to hold,

Satirical view of Lincoln's secret journey from Harrisburg to Washington, February 23, 1861. Drawn by Adalbert John Volck, a Baltimore dentist who possessed extraordinary skill as a draftsman. Volck was an ardent Confederate sympathizer.

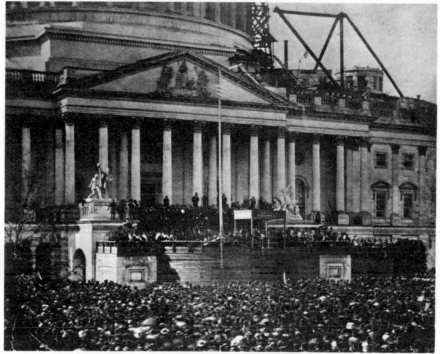

CHICAGO HISTORICAL SOCIETY

The inauguration of Lincoln, March 4, 1861

occupy, and possess the property, and places belonging to the government, and to collect the duties and imposts; but beyond what may be necessary for these objects, there will be no invasion—no using of force against, or among the people anywhere."

Lincoln closed with the emotional appeal that made his address forever memorable. "We are not enemies, but friends. We must not be enemies. Though passion may have strained, it must not break our bonds of affection. The mystic chords of memory, stretching from every battle-field and patriot grave, to every living heart and hearthstone, all over this broad land, will yet swell the chorus of the Union, when again touched, as surely they will be, by the better angles of our nature."

The newly-inaugurated President pleads for reconciliation between North and South

Moving as it was, the inaugural offered no plan for resolving the national crisis and spelled out no compromise. In essence it did express the hope that with time the disaffected South, realizing that the new Administration posed no threat to slavery where it already existed, would retreat from the extreme position it had assumed.

But there would be no time. As the Southern states had seceded, their local troops had seized nearly all the Federal forts within their boundaries or off their shores. Only five remained in the hands of the

33

1 In compliance with a custom as old as the government itself, I appear before you
2 to address you briefly, and to take, in your presence, the oath prescribed by the Con-
3 stitution of the United States, to be taken by the President "before he enters on the
4 execution of his office."

5 The more modern custom of electing a Chief Magistrate upon a previously declared
6 platform of principles, supercedes, in a great measure, the necessity of re-stating those
7 principles in an address of this sort. Upon the plainest grounds of good faith, one so
8 elected is not at liberty to shift his position. It is necessarily implied, if not ex-
9 pressed, that, in his judgment, the platform which he thus accepts, binds him to
10 nothing either unconstitutional or inexpedient.

11 Having been so elected upon the Chicago Platform, and while I would repeat noth-
12 ing in it, of aspersion or epithet or question of motive against any man or party, I
13 hold myself bound by duty, as well as impelled by inclination to follow, within the
14 executive sphere, the principles therein declared. By no other course could I meet
15 the reasonable expectations of the country.

16 I do not consider it necessary at present for me to say more than I have, in relation
17 to those matters of administration, about which there is no special excitement.

18 Apprehension seems to exist among the people of the Southern States, that by
19 the accession of a Republican Administration, their property, and their peace, and per-
20 sonal security, are to be endangered. There has never been any reasonable cause for such
21 apprehension. Indeed, the most ample evidence to the contrary has all the while ex-
22 isted, and been open to their inspection. It is found in nearly all the published
23 speeches of him who now addresses you. I do but quote from one of those speeches
24 when I declare that "I have no purpose, directly or indirectly, to interfere with the
25 institution of slavery in the States where it exists. I believe I have no lawful right
26 to do so, and I have no inclination to do so." Those who nominated and elected me
27 did so with full knowledge that I had made this, and many similar declarations,
28 and had never recanted them. And more than this, they placed in the platform, for
29 my acceptance, and as a law to themselves, and to me, the clear and emphatic resolu-
30 tion which I now read :

31 "Resolved, That the maintenance inviolate of the rights of the States, and espe-
32 cially the right of each State to order and control its own domestic institutions accord-
33 ing to its own judgment exclusively, is essential to that balance of power on which
34 the perfection and endurance of our political fabric depend; and we denounce the
35 lawless invasion by armed force of the soil of any State or Territory, no matter under
36 what pretext, as among the gravest of crimes."

*The first page of Lincoln's Inaugural Address
as he had it printed before leaving Springfield*

Union: Fort Jefferson in the Dry Tortugas, Fort Pickens in Pensacola Bay, Fort Taylor at Key West, Fort Monroe at Hampton Roads, and Fort Sumter in Charleston Harbor. On March 5, Lincoln's first full day in office, he was presented with a shocking fact. Major Anderson in Fort Sumter had provisions for no more than thirty days. If he did not receive additional supplies within a month he would have to surrender. Lincoln had been aware, of course, of the fact that the Buchanan administration, two months earlier, had sent an unarmed merchant ship, *The Star of the West,* with provisions and additional troops to Sumter, but that she had turned back when fired upon by the shore batteries. He had not suspected, however, that the situation was as critical as he now discovered it to be.

Could Sumter be reinforced? Lincoln's military advisers answered that it could not be relieved or even provisioned without an army of 20,000 men and a bloody battle. There were not 20,000 men in the Regular Army of the United States, and if there had been, they could not have been assembled and transported to the danger point in time.

FLORIDA

CHICAGO HISTORICAL SOCIETY

Robert Anderson. This photograph, made in 1861, shows him wearing the single star of a brigadier general, a rank to which he was promoted on May 15, 1861.

Thomas Jonathan Jackson, graduate of West Point, veteran of the Mexican War, and Professor of Artillery Tactics and Natural Philosophy at the Virginia Military Institute.

Pierre Gustave Toutant Beauregard. Commissioned a brigadier general in the Confederate Army on March 1, 1861, he commanded the troops that fired the opening shots of the war.

GEORGIA

Naval officers, who held shore batteries in low esteem, were more optimistic, but even if they were correct, an attempt to relieve the fort would be almost certain to precipitate war.

As the only apparent alternative, should Sumter be surrendered? (Southern "commissioners" were even then in Washington attempting to negotiate the transfer of the forts still in possession of the Union to the Confederacy.) When confronted with this question, a majority of the Cabinet favored surrender. Lincoln, never one to move hastily, deferred a decision. Within two or three weeks he realized that to the North the fort in Charleston Harbor had become a symbol. To surrender it would be equivalent to consenting to a dissolution of the Union. By this time a majority of his Cabinet had swung around to the same view. Lincoln's attitude was strengthened by the reports of emissaries whom he had sent to Charleston. In their opinion the people of South Carolina were adamant in their desire to break up the Union and were no less firm in their determination that Fort Sumter should pass from the hands of the Federal government to the Confederacy.

Time pressed. Finally Lincoln made a decision in between relief and abandonment. He would send provisions but no troops to Anderson. On April 6 he dispatched a messenger to Francis W. Pickens, who had succeeded William H. Gist as Governor of South Carolina. "I am directed by the President of the United States," the message read, "to notify you to expect an attempt will be made to supply Fort Sumter with provisions only; and that, if such attempt be not resisted, no effort to throw in men, arms, or ammunition, will be made, without further notice, or in case of an attack upon the Fort."

Immediately upon receipt of this notification Pickens relayed it to Jefferson Davis at Montgomery. After an anxious cabinet meeting, L. P. Walker, the Confederate Secretary of War, ordered General P. G. T. Beauregard, in command at Charleston, to demand the evacuation of the fort and if this were refused to take it by force. On April 11 Beauregard sent his demand for surrender to Anderson. Anderson refused it but remarked that he would be forced by lack of provisions to give up the fort in a few days. To Beauregard the reply was unsatisfactory. At 3:30 A.M. on April 12 he notified the Federal commander that he would open fire within an hour. True to his promise a mortar fired the first shot at 4:30.

The engagement lasted for thirty-three hours. Although many of Sumter's guns were put out of commission and its interior burned, none of the defenders was killed. Near the end of the battle, the relief expedition appeared at the mouth of the harbor but made no effort to come to the aid of the beleaguered fort. With his ammunition nearly exhausted and his provisions gone, Anderson surrendered. Beauregard

NEW YORK HISTORICAL SOCIETY

Francis W. Pickens, Governor of South Carolina, who willingly guided the events that his predecessor, William H. Gist, had set in motion.

Outfitting a Confederate volunteer.

From a water color by W. L. Sheppard.

permitted the garrison to embark on the ships of the expedition and to salute the Stars and Stripes. Ironically the gun firing the salute exploded and killed a Union soldier, the only casualty of the first battle of the war.

Shock and anger at the assault on Sumter and chagrin at its surrender swept the North. Offers of unlimited support poured into Washington. One of the most welcome was that tendered by Lincoln's longtime rival, Stephen A. Douglas. On the evening of April 14 he called on the President to say that while he remained unalterably opposed to the Administration on all political issues, he would sustain the government in preserving the Union. "The capital of our country is in danger," he said, "and must be protected at all hazards, at any expense of men and money."

Lincoln responded to the Confederate challenge by issuing three proclamations. The first, dated April 15, called up 75,000 militia

38

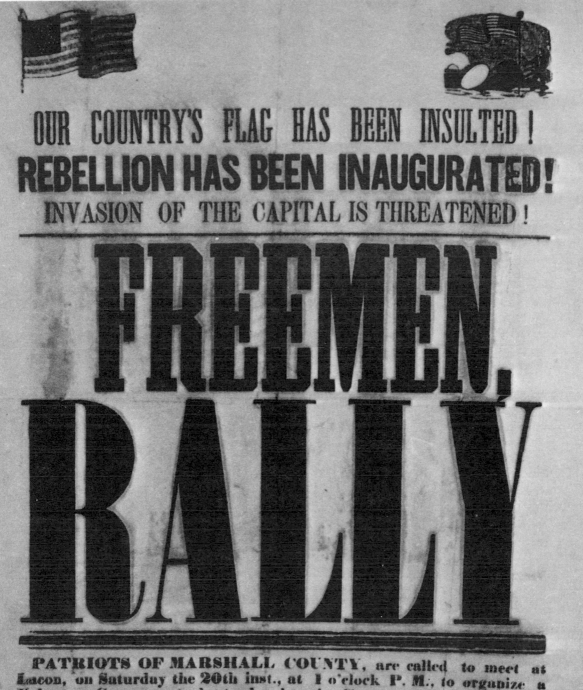

OUR COUNTRY'S FLAG HAS BEEN INSULTED !
REBELLION HAS BEEN INAUGURATED!
INVASION OF THE CAPITAL IS THREATENED !

FREEMEN, RALLY

PATRIOTS OF MARSHALL COUNTY, are called to meet at Lacon, on Saturday the 20th inst., at 1 o'clock P. M., to organize a Volunteer Company, to be tendered to the Government to support the *Constitution* and the *Laws,* in answer to the President's call.

"To Arms, to Arms ye Braves—
Our God and our Country."

Lacon, April 18th, A. D. 1861.

Poster of a war rally at Lacon, Illinois

The Baltimore Riot. The dentist-artist A. J. Volck pictured the mob—patriots in his eyes—attacking the 6th Massachusetts.

Camp Defiance was established at Cairo, Illinois, at the juncture of the Ohio and Mississippi rivers, as soon as troops could be rushed there after the capitulation of Fort Sumter.

REGULATIONS FOR
CAMP DEFIANCE

Reveille at	5
Breakfast Call at	7
Guard Mounting at	9½
Dinner Call at	12
Company Drills from	1 to 3
Dress Parade at	6
Tattoo at	9
Taps at	10

1. All non-commissioned Officers will be within the Camp at 8 P. M.

2. No commissioned Officer will be allowed to remain out of the Camp after Tattoo, without the permission of his Battalion Commander.

3. After 8 P. M. no loud singing, no cheering or firing arms will be allowed, nor any firing or cheering on the Sabbath. The Commandant requests that the troops will observe the Sabbath in an orderly and Christian-like manner.

4. Citizens visiting the Camp must obtain a written pass from Head Quarters.

5. Guards, when recognizing Staff Officers and commissioned Officers of the line, will pass them, in the daylight, without the countersign.

The Commandant will hold the various commanders strictly accountable to the observance of the above.

By order of

B. M. PRENTISS, Commandant.

from the various states. At the same time, calls for troops were sent to the governors of those states which had not seceded. On April 19 a second proclamation announced that all Southern ports would be blockaded. Two weeks later, in a third proclamation, the President called for 42,000 three-year volunteers for the Regular Army and for 18,000 volunteers to serve from one to three years in the Navy. He had no warrant in law to increase the size of either the Army or Navy but he counted on Congress to validate his action when it met.

The means immediately available to the President for suppressing rebellion were slender. Since the War of 1812 the United States had seen no need for a standing army larger than was necessary to keep peace along the advancing frontier. In 1861 the Regular Army consisted of 13,000 men, most of whom were dispersed in far distant posts. The Army's efficiency had recently been impaired by the resignation of hundreds of career officers whose sympathies lay with the South. It was obvious that the war to come must be fought by volunteers.

Most of the responses to the Administration's call for troops promised immediate compliance, but a few were contemptuous. The Governor of Kentucky replied that his state would furnish no troops "for the wicked purpose of subduing her sister Southern States." "You can get no troops from North Carolina," her governor wired. Claiborne Fox Jackson, Governor of Missouri, telegraphed that the Federal requisition was "illegal, unconstitutional, and revolutionary in its object, inhuman and diabolical, and cannot be complied with." Tennessee would not furnish a single man "for purpose of coercion, but 50,000, if necessary, for the defense of our rights and those of our southern brethren." To similar requisitions from the Confederate Secretary of War the governors of the seceded states promised to respond with all the volunteers they could equip.

In crossroads villages, as well as big cities, drums beat, fifes shrilled, and men lined up to sign muster rolls. Everywhere, meetings whipped up the war spirit. In Galena, Illinois, the lead-mining town in the northwestern corner of the state, a company of volunteers enlisted at a mass meeting. The citizens wanted a former Regular Army officer named Ulysses S. Grant, who had resigned his commission under a cloud and was clerking in his father's leather shop, to take command of the company. Grant refused, but offered to drill the recruits and accompany them to the state capital. At Milwaukee three volunteer rifle companies were formed in one day. Michigan cities subscribed $100,000 to buy equipment for the state's first troops. On April 16 New Orleans sent two volunteer companies to Pensacola and word came that regiments were forming throughout the state. At the Virginia Military Institute at Lexington, Major Thomas Jonathan Jackson, Professor of Artillery Tactics and Natural Philosophy, knelt for private

41

*The White House. In this building, then called the Executive
Mansion, Lincoln anxiously awaited the arrival of Union troops.*

prayers and then led his company of cadets to the railroad station to
entrain for Richmond. In hundreds of cities, both North and South,
tailors whipped up uniforms and women sewed flags to be presented
to local companies and regiments. In such ways a peaceful people
sprang to arms.

As soon as possible the hastily organized troops were sent to strategic points. Regiments from Chicago garrisoned Cairo at the junction
of the Ohio and Mississippi rivers. Ohio troops moved toward western
Virginia. Southern levies were sent to Tennessee, where they could
move north to join with Kentucky if that state should abandon the
neutral position which she had assumed. Other Southern forces threatened Harpers Ferry and concentrated in Virginia near the national
capital.

For the North, the point of supreme importance was Washington. At all costs the city must be secured against Southern invasion.
Governor John A. Andrew of Massachusetts, who had estimated the
gravity of the situation earlier than any of the other Union governors,
had several regiments in readiness. On April 17, the 6th Massachusetts entrained for Washington. Two days later the train carrying
the regiment pulled into Baltimore. There a mile separated the station
at which it arrived and the station from which it would have to depart.
During the transfer the troops were attacked by a pro-Southern mob.
In the fighting that followed, four soldiers and twelve civilians were
killed. To send additional troops through the city appeared to be
impossible, and Washington was isolated from the rest of the country.

42

Days passed before a route around Baltimore was opened. The President—in fact all loyal inhabitants—lived in continual apprehension. One afternoon Lincoln walked the floor of his office, looked wistfully out of the window, and exclaimed with anguish, "Why don't they come! Why don't they come!" At last on April 25, six days after the riot, the 7th New York Infantry arrived, formed at the railroad station, and marched up Pennsylvania Avenue to the White House. Nicolay and Hay, Lincoln's secretaries, caught the excitement of the event:

"As they passed up the magnificent street, with their well-formed ranks, their exact military step, their soldierly bearing, their gayly floating flags, and the inspiring music of their splendid regimental band, they seemed to sweep all thought of danger and all taint of treason out of that great national thoroughfare and out of every human heart in the Federal city. The presence of this single regiment seemed to turn the scales of fate. Cheer upon cheer greeted them; windows were thrown up; houses opened; the population came forth upon the streets as for a holiday. It was an epoch in American history. For the first time, the combined spirit and power of liberty entered the nation's capital."

By the early summer of 1861 both North and South had raised and organized thousands of troops. Many were without uniforms, most poorly armed, and few were well trained, but in these respects neither side had an advantage over the other. By this time, too, the political

Colonel Elmer Ellsworth, second from left, commanded one of the first regiments to reach Washington, the New York Fire Zouaves. Ellsworth was killed on May 24, 1861, at Alexandria, Virginia, after he had cut down a Confederate flag flying there.

Lieutenant General Winfield Scott.
From a photograph made in 1862.

Major General Irvin McDowell.
First Bull Run was his bad luck.

situation had stabilized. Through the energetic action of Union men in St. Louis, a Confederate threat to that city had been checkmated and the state prevented from seceding. Kentucky, it was apparent, had given up its hope of neutrality and would remain in the Union. Maryland, where secession sentiment had been strong, would also remain loyal. On the other hand Virginia, Arkansas, Tennessee, and North Carolina had passed ordinances of secession and joined the Confederate States of America. Minor military movements had taken place in western Virginia where George B. McClellan, commanding Union troops, won a reputation out of all proportion to the forces involved and the importance of the campaign. His success, however, led the loyal element in that part of the state to organize a Union government and inaugurate the movement that would lead to the formation of the state of West Virginia.

By midsummer North and South had been at war for over two months, yet no action of consequence had taken place. From the beginning, Northerners had assumed that one big battle would bring an end to the rebellion. Now, with thousands of troops encamped in the vicinity of Washington, the time had come to strike. The Confederacy had decided to transfer its seat of government from Montgomery to Richmond, Virginia, where its Congress would meet on July 20. Northern newspapers demanded action. Horace Greeley's New York *Tribune,* the most influential journal in the country, spoke for millions when day after day it carried at the head of its editorial column the appeal:

"Forward to Richmond! Forward to Richmond! The Rebel Congress must not be allowed to meet there on the 20th of July! By that date the place must be held by the National Army!"

Lincoln, skilled in interpreting public opinion, summoned a cabinet meeting attended by several generals to consider a campaign against the Confederate forces massed at and around Manassas Junction, twenty-five miles west of Washington. General Winfield Scott, veteran of the War of 1812 and hero of the Mexican War, still at seventy-five Commander of the United States Army, demurred. Federal troops were green and none of their officers had deployed more than a regiment or two in battle. To this contention the answer was made that the Confederates suffered under the same disadvantages. Scott, a Virginian but loyal to the Union, yielded and agreed to the advance. It should be commanded, he specified, by General Irvin McDowell, who had spent all of his mature life in the Regular Army. McDowell counted his own forces at 35,000 men with a reserve of

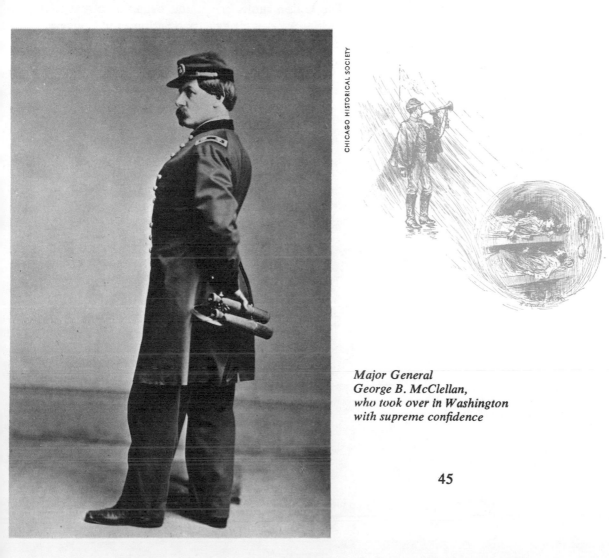

CHICAGO HISTORICAL SOCIETY

Major General
George B. McClellan,
who took over in Washington
with supreme confidence

45

10,000. The Confederates, he estimated, numbered approximately 25,000. Their positions around Centreville and along Bull Run were not formidable. The success of the operation as Scott and McDowell saw it depended upon preventing a Confederate force near Harpers Ferry under General Joseph E. Johnston from joining the main Confederate Army before or during McDowell's attack. General Robert Patterson, a superannuated veteran of the War of 1812 and the Mexican War, was entrusted with this responsibility.

McDowell began his advance on July 16 but moved forward cautiously. The Confederate authorities, well informed of Union troop movements, immediately ordered Johnston to come to the support of Beauregard, in command at Manassas. Johnston succeeded in deluding Patterson and started his brigades to the scene of action.

McDowell struck on Sunday, July 21, with as much of his force as he could maneuver. At first the battle went in his favor, giving him sufficient confidence to wire Scott that victory could be expected. The old general lay down to take a nap and Lincoln went for a ride in his carriage. But then portions of Johnston's army arrived on the battlefield and the tide turned. The Union ranks broke and began a retreat that ended in a rout. Many threw away their arms and rations and staggered back to Washington in panic. Congressmen and other Washingtonians who had driven to the battlefield in the expectation of witnessing a gladiatorial combat that would end the war whipped their horses back

CHICAGO HISTORICAL SOCIETY

Major General John C. Frémont. In Missouri, military pomp and power went to his head.

46

*Grant at Cairo in the fall of 1861. He stands to
the left of the man in front of the center pillar.*

to the capital with all the celerity of which they were capable. Scott,
awakened from his nap, was at first incredulous. Lincoln, though
sorely disappointed, refused to panic. By Monday it was apparent that
the Confederates were making no pursuit and that the safety of Washington was not threatened. The Union War Department soon reported:
"Our loss is much less than was at first represented, and the troops
have reached the forts in much better condition than we expected. . . .
the capital is safe."

Bull Run shook the North from its complacency. It was obvious that
instead of being over in a day the war would stretch out for months   *The Union defeat*
and perhaps years. Governors offered troops and sent forward regi-   *at Bull Run*
ments recruited to full strength. Where the first enlistments had been   *promises a long war*
for ninety days, now men were signed up for three years or the duration
of the war. It was apparent, too, that a shakeup of the Union command was a necessity. Scott was too old and too infirm to take the
field. McDowell had forfeited his chance for supreme command even
though the defeat at Bull Run was not altogether his fault. On the
military scene one man seemed to stand above all others. George B.

47

Charles Wilkes, impetuous captain of the San Jacinto

McClellan, holding a major general's commission from the Governor of Ohio, looked to his contemporaries as the coming Napoleon. He had graduated from West Point in 1846, ranking second in his class. In the Mexican War he had won three brevets for meritorious conduct. In 1857 he had resigned from the Army to accept the vice presidency of the Illinois Central Railroad and early in 1860 had become president of the Ohio and Mississippi Railroad. Upon the outbreak of the war he had offered himself to his state.

McClellan's victories in western Virginia had been small affairs but at least they were victories. When called to Washington immediately after Bull Run he responded brimming with confidence. In letters to his wife he wrote of the adulation of the public and was injudicious enough to express the contempt which he quickly came to feel for the President and his own elderly superior. "The people called upon me to save the country," he wrote, "I must save it and I cannot respect anything that is in the way."

To Bull Run the South reacted differently. The victory reinforced the prevailing opinion that the Confederacy needed only to repel advancing Union armies and to wait until the North tired of the war. Enlistments fell off sharply. Soldiering, the young hotheads from the plantations had discovered, was a dreary business: drill, spit-and-polish, discipline, and drill again. As one Alabama enlisted man discovered: "A soldier is worse than any negro on Chatahooche river. He has no privileges whatever. He is under worse taskmasters than any negro. He is not treated with any respect whatever. His officers may insult him and he has no right to open his mouth and dare not do it." Besides, with the military tide running as it had started, there might be little need for more men.

Soldiering turns out to be something less than a picnic

Congress, having been called in special session by the President, went about the work of organizing the Union for victory. In his message of July 4, 1861, the President had asked for 400,000 men and $400,000,000. The response was quick. During the session Congress authorized a loan not to exceed $250,000,000, passed the first income tax ever levied by the United States Government, and increased tariff duties. On the other side the Confederate Congress, in session at Richmond, levied direct taxes upon real estate, slaves, and other property.

Both Union and Confederacy prepare for a long war

For McClellan in Washington the first duty would be to reorganize the troops, demoralized in their first battle, and to train the new levies that were pouring into the capital. This task would preclude offensive operations for months. In the West, however, green troops were spoiling for a fight. In southwestern Missouri and nearby Arkansas a Confederate army of about 10,000 had been assembled. To Nathaniel Lyon, a Regular Army captain who had been advanced to the rank of brigadier general and who now commanded the Union troops in Missouri, the presence of the Confederate force was intolerable. Lyon, with no more than 6000 men, attacked the Confederates at Wilson's Creek near Springfield on the early morning of August 10. At first his audacity was rewarded, but as the hours passed, the weight of superior numbers made itself felt. The result was a sharp Union defeat in which Lyon lost his life.

Although the battle of Wilson's Creek would be the only military engagement of any importance in Missouri for several months, the state soon posed a problem of the utmost embarrassment to Lincoln. While Lyon was in the field, John C. Frémont was put in charge of the Military Department of the West with headquarters at St. Louis. In Republican circles at least, no man was more popular than this gallant explorer who had been his party's first candidate for the Presidency. Events soon showed, however, that personal bravery and a romantic career left something to be desired as far as his new responsibilities were concerned. Rumors of extravagance and even corruption swelled. These alone might not have been fatal, but Frémont allowed his own sense of importance to go to his head and issued a proclamation that invoked martial law, confiscated the property of all Missourians who had taken up arms against the national government, and freed their slaves. The act made him the idol of the anti-slavery people of the North. Lincoln saw the situation differently. Frémont's proclamation could easily drive the border states, now leaning to the Union, to secession and would infuriate thousands of the loyal Democrats who had been assured by the President that they were fighting a war for the restoration of the Union and not for the abolition of slavery. Lincoln, in a calm and considerate letter, asked Frémont to withdraw, as of his own motion, his proclamation of emancipation. Frémont refused, sending his response to Washington by his wife, a strong-minded and outspoken woman. Lincoln thereupon revoked the emancipation clause of the proclamation and modified the confiscation edict. Vituperation from the anti-slavery press and anti-slavery leaders was his reward. When Frémont continued to demonstrate that the administrative duties of his post were beyond his ability and gave other evidences of insubordination, he was relieved but kept on active service.

Early in November, Missouri once more took the spotlight. U. S. Grant, who had drilled the volunteers at Galena and had later been given a colonel's commission and the command of the 21st Illinois Infantry, had become Brigadier General Grant and commanded a force at Paducah, Kentucky. A Confederate army under the former Episcopal Bishop, Leonidas Polk, occupied Columbus, at the western end of Kentucky on the Mississippi River. In Missouri, Frémont, still in charge, had begun a slow and timorous movement to the west. To prevent the Confederates at Columbus from interfering with his movement he asked Grant to create a diversion in his favor. Taking 3000 men in several steamers, Grant occupied the town of Belmont opposite Columbus. To his surprise he found that the Confederates were already there in numbers, well armed and entrenched. A sharp battle followed and Grant had to retreat to his transports to escape either capture or annihilation. To his father he wrote that the expedition had accomplished its purpose and more. But it was a narrow escape and not a propitious beginning for the newly commissioned general.

Ulysses S. Grant, on the way up, narrowly escapes disaster

In the East, McClellan continued to drill his troops while the people of the North began to wonder audibly when he was going to use the army that he was creating. The general's initial popularity waned rapidly. Ball's Bluff, an inconsequential engagement in October, 1861, sent it skidding faster. Colonel Edward D. Baker, one of Lincoln's oldest and closest friends, had been authorized to make a "slight demonstration" against Confederate forces on the Potomac not far from Washington. Through inept generalship the Union forces were severely whipped and Baker was killed.

Soon after Fort Sumter, Lincoln had proclaimed a blockade of all the Confederate ports. In the beginning, the Union Navy was clearly

*Prince Albert, consort of Queen
Victoria. His moderation helped
to prevent war between the
United States and Great Britain.*

unequal to the task. At the time of Lincoln's inauguration Union naval vessels of all classes numbered only ninety and of these only forty-two were in commission. Many were obsolete sailing ships which would have to be extensively overhauled before they would be of much use, while others were on foreign stations from which they could not be recalled quickly.

Nevertheless, the Administration went to work vigorously to create a navy. Gideon Welles, Lincoln's Secretary of the Navy, had had little relevant experience and his luxuriant white beard and toupee made him an easy target for ridicule. But with his capable assistant, Gustavus V. Fox, Welles worked wonders. Merchant ships were bought or chartered and the keels of new vessels laid. By July 4, eighty-two ships were in commission and by the end of the year the number had risen to two hundred sixty-four. The blockade grew steadily in effectiveness although many blockade-runners still slipped in and out of Southern ports. The Union Navy faced the task of closing these ports one by one until the commerce of the Confederacy with the world at large was strangled.

*The Union creates
a formidable Navy*

One of the first targets was Port Royal, which guarded the harbor of Beaufort, South Carolina, about halfway between Charleston and Savannah. In mid-October a naval expedition commanded by Flag Officer Samuel F. du Pont left New York Harbor. Transports carrying troops joined the fleet off Old Point Comfort, Virginia. On November 7, Du Pont's ships opened fire on the defending forts, Beauregard and

51

Walker. The troops landed only to find that the garrisons had slipped away. The victory, the first to be credited to the Union Navy, gave the sagging morale of the North a strong lift.

The Navy, or rather an impetuous naval officer, would soon have a hand in an episode of far greater importance than the closing of a Confederate port. In October the Confederate government decided to send James M. Mason of Virginia to London and John Slidell of Louisiana to Paris, where they were to work for the recognition of the Confederacy. The two men ran the blockade to Havana, Cuba, and there took passage on the British mail steamer *Trent*. On November 8 Captain Charles Wilkes of the U.S.S. *San Jacinto* stopped the *Trent*, took off the two commissioners and their secretaries and carried them as prisoners to Fort Warren in Boston Harbor. When news of the seizure became known, Wilkes was hailed as a hero throughout the North. In England both government and public flared with anger. Under international law Wilkes, who had acted without authority, had no right to search the British ship and arrest the agents without bringing the ship into port for adjudication. The British ministry drafted a hot demand for an apology and the immediate release of Mason and

Lincoln and Prince Albert calm the hotheads, and the United States evades war with Great Britain

Slidell. Queen Victoria's husband, Prince Albert, then on his deathbed, succeeded in toning down the demand and the British minister in Washington presented it with tact. Although Seward, the Secretary of State, wanted to defy the British and although public opinion in the North was strong in favor of such a course, Lincoln took the opposite position. He saw that the British were relying on principles which the United States had gone to war to defend in 1812, and he also realized that in 1861 the country could not court a second and simultaneous conflict. The prisoners were released and normal relations between the two nations restored.

McClellan takes command of the Union armies

As the year came to a close, General Scott asked to be relieved of his command and McClellan assumed full control of the Union armies. The forces in the field for the North approached 200,000 men. More than half of that number were encamped in the vicinity of Washington. Other armies held Harpers Ferry, Virginia; Paducah, Kentucky; and Cairo, Illinois. The largest Confederate concentration was in northern Virginia, west and south of Washington, but smaller forces occupied points in northern Tennessee. In spite of the naval blockade, Charleston, South Carolina; Wilmington, North Carolina; Savannah, Georgia; Mobile, Alabama; Galveston, Texas; and New Orleans remained fairly easy of access. Shortages of food and clothing began to be evident in the South, but on the whole life behind the lines in both sections of the divided country proceeded much as usual.

Fort Moultrie, from which Major Robert Anderson withdrew on December 26, 1860, in order to garrison Fort Sumter

Arsenal Yard at Charleston in 1865 at the close of the war

The East Battery, Charleston

A postwar view of Harpers Ferry, at the confluence of the Potomac and Shenandoah rivers. The town changed hands often.

The Norfolk Navy Yard. On April 20, 1861 the Union Navy Department ordered its abandonment and destruction. The seated figure is Alfred R. Waud, noted battle artist.

*The Charleston Light Artillery, 1863. War, in
those early days, called for considerable strutting.*

*Sergeant Francis E. Brownell, 11th New
York Volunteers. On May 24, 1861, he
killed James T. Jackson, who had assassi-
nated Elmer Ellsworth.*

*Abram Duryée, commissioned colonel of the
5th New York Infantry on April 25, 1861.
His uniform illustrated the individuality of
the early volunteers.*

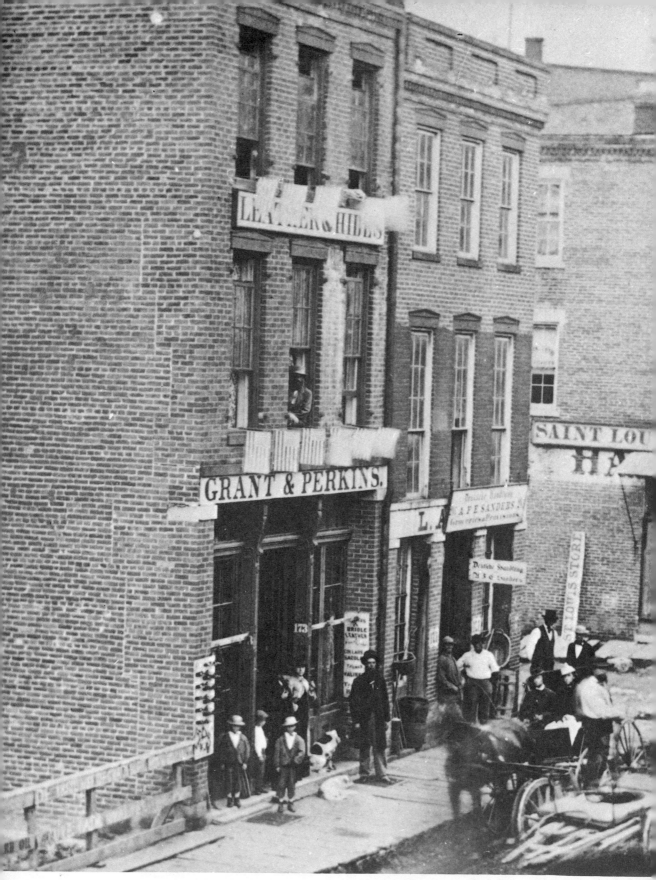

Ulysses S. Grant, U.S. Military Academy, 1843, and a veteran of the Mexican War, left this unpretentious store in Galena, Illinois, to serve on the staff of Governor Richard Yates, and soon afterward, to take command of the 21st Illinois Infantry, a fractious regiment.

*An example of the
primitive state of
the Southern economy*

*As the Union troops moved into Alexandria, Virginia,
where Ellsworth was killed, they saw slave pens like this.*

Volck, the Baltimore artist, offered a satirical picture of the enlistment of Daniel E. Sickles' Excelsior Brigade, New York, in June, 1861. Sickles, who had killed his wife's lover in 1859, was an easy target.

War meeting

Charles W. Reed drew a vivid sketch of a Union war rally. Fervid oratory induced many a young man to sign the muster roll.

Again Volck dipped his pen in acid. This time his subject was the German-American, Franz Sigel, who rallied large numbers of Germans to the cause of the Union but fought without distinction. Nevertheless, "I fights mit Sigel," was the proud slogan of his soldiers.

Centreville, Virginia, in 1862. As McDowell advanced toward Manassas in the First Bull Run Campaign, the Confederates withdrew from this little town twenty-five miles west and south of Washington.

McDowell's advancing men discovered that the Confederate defenses at Centreville were less formidable than they appeared. "Quaker guns"—tree trunks—contributed to the illusion of strength. An 1862 view.

59

Burnside's brigade opening First Bull Run. Alfred R. Waud,
the artist, was in the field for the New York Illustrated News.

This 1880's view shows a house built over the foundation of the Henry House,
destroyed in 1862. Near this house during First Bull Run, Jackson's Virginia
brigade held the line that won for him the sobriquet "Stonewall."

Parrott guns of the 1st New York Artillery. These rifled cannon—20-pounders are shown here—were much superior to the smoothbore Napoleons, the basic field artillery weapon of both armies.

Nathaniel Lyon, killed at Wilson's Creek, August 10, 1861

NO COMPROMISE WITH TRAITORS, AND NO ARGUMENT BUT A KNOCK-DOWN ARGUMENT.

Volunteers Wanted!
FOR COMPANY M,
COLONEL OWEN'S 2d REGIMENT,
BAKER'S BRIGADE!

This is an excellent opportunity for Young Men to serve in this Company. The Officers have been in active service since the commencement of the Rebellion, and understand their duty.

PAY AND RATIONS BEGIN WHEN ENROLLED.

Regim'l Head Quarters, 421 Walnut St.
COMPANY HEAD QUARTERS, Richmond St. above Palmer, Philadelphia.

JOHN DOYLE,   1st Lieut.
JOHN McQUILLIN, 2d   MARTIN CALLINAN FROST, Captain.

KING & BAIRD, Printers, No. 607 Sansom Street, Philadelphia.

Volunteers Wanted for Baker's Brigade. Edward D. Baker, a close friend of Lincoln, was killed at Ball's Bluff, October 21, 1861.

After First Bull Run, the North recruited with frenzy. Shown here: a war rally at the little town of Momence in northeastern Illinois.

"Up, Patriots, and at Them" in the 49th Ohio Volunteers.

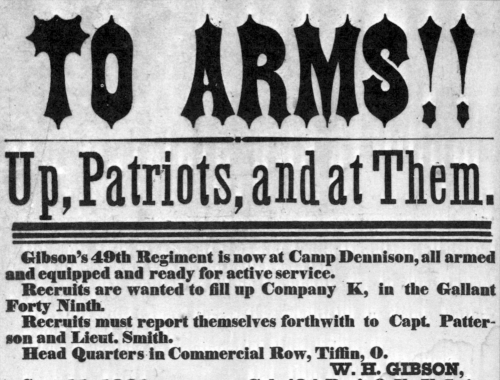

TO ARMS!!
Up, Patriots, and at Them.

Gibson's 49th Regiment is now at Camp Dennison, all armed and equipped and ready for active service.

Recruits are wanted to fill up Company K, in the Gallant Forty Ninth.

Recruits must report themselves forthwith to Capt. Patterson and Lieut. Smith.

Head Quarters in Commercial Row, Tiffin, O.

W. H. GIBSON,

Sept. 11, 1861.　　　Col. 49th Reg't O. V., U. S. A.

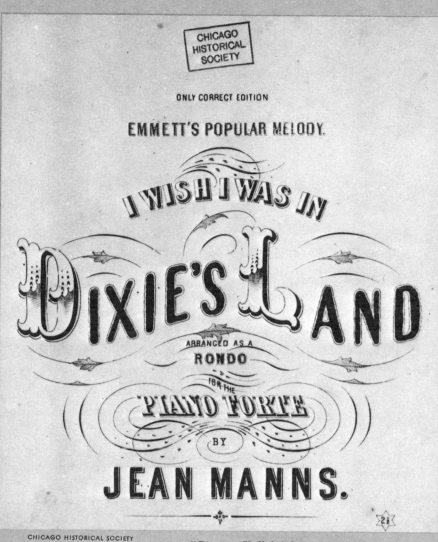

ONLY CORRECT EDITION

EMMETT'S POPULAR MELODY.

I WISH I WAS IN

Dixie's Land

ARRANGED AS A
RONDO
FOR THE
PIANO FORTE
BY

JEAN MANNS.

Stirring music brought in recruits. The South made "Dixie," a minstrel song written by a Northerner, its own.

"Glory, Hallelujah," or "John Brown's Body." With words that Julia Ward Howe would write in 1862, it would become "The Battle Hymn of the Republic."

"Sons of the South awake to glory, A thousand voices bid you rise."

THE
SOUTHERN
MARSEILLAISE.

NEW ORLEANS:
A. E. BLACKMAR & BRO, 74 CAMP STREET.

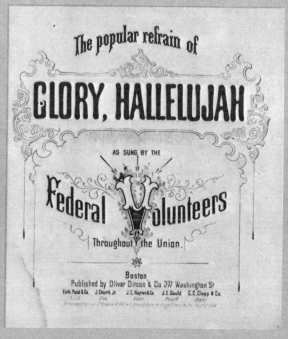

The popular refrain of

GLORY, HALLELUJAH

AS SUNG BY THE

Federal Volunteers

Throughout the Union.

Boston
Published by Oliver Ditson & Co 277 Washington St
Firth Pond & Co.   J. Church Jr.   J. C. Haynes & Co.   J. E. Gould   C. C. Clapp & Co.

On August 29, 1861, U.S. Army and Navy forces under Admiral Silas H. Stringham and Colonel Rush C. Hawkins captured Forts Hatteras and Clark in Hatteras Inlet, North Carolina. Alfred R. Waud pictured the action.

"We are a band of brothers
And native to the soil
Fighting for the property
We gained by honest toil."

A Union victory far more important than Hatteras took place on November 7, 1861, when a fleet under Flag Officer Samuel Francis du Pont (shown here) and 12,000 troops commanded by Brigadier General Thomas W. Sherman ("the other Sherman") captured Forts Beauregard and Walker in Port Royal Sound, South Carolina.

Before the end of 1861 blockade-running had become a highly profitable and highly hazardous occupation. Shown here, at an unidentified port, is the blockade-runner Old Dominion.

At Mound City, Illinois, on the Ohio River six miles above its junction with the Mississippi, the Union located marine ways which kept the boats of the western river fleet in repair.

Early in the war the Lincoln administration began arresting civilians suspected of disloyalty. Many were held in the Old Capitol Prison in Washington. The building had been hastily erected as a replacement for the Capitol, burned by the British in the War of 1812.

The "Mess Boy," filling canteens, was the subject of a water color by the Southern artist, W. L. Sheppard.

The amenities of civilized living prevailed in the North as well as the South. Alfred R. Waud sketched a Thanksgiving dinner, November 28, 1861, in a Union army camp.

BITTER AND BLOODY
FIGHTING

I N WASHINGTON, Lincoln and other Administration leaders had
difficulty containing their impatience. McClellan professed to be
anxious to move against the Confederates, but he had allowed a warm
autumn and an early open winter to go by without action. By his
delay McClellan revealed for the first time one of his weaknesses as
a commander: he overestimated the strength of his opponents. At the
end of October, 1861, he had reported to the Secretary of War that
Joseph E. Johnston, commanding the Confederate armies before him,
had 150,000 men and that an army of 240,000 would therefore be
required to attack him. In point of fact, at that time Johnston commanded 41,000 effectives. Six weeks later McClellan estimated that
Johnston could meet him with "equal forces nearly." The Confederate
commander then had 47,000 men, less than one-third of the number
in McClellan's army. Johnston, a fifty-four-year-old Regular Army
officer whose abilities Jefferson Davis never appreciated, was quite
content. Almost in sight of the Federal capital, he could drill and
discipline his men and neutralize a much larger enemy force merely
by staying where he was. In the late summer and early fall of 1861
the daily report of "all quiet on the Potomac" had been a reassuring
phrase in Washington. By the end of the year it had become a taunt.
Late in December, McClellan became seriously ill with typhoid

McClellan reveals
a serious fault:
he consistently
overestimates
Confederate strength

fever. Lincoln, restive as he was, could do nothing. By mid-January, 1862, when it was obvious that the general was on the road to recovery, the President came to the end of his patience. In a conference with ranking Union generals he commented that if McClellan did not want to use the Army of the Potomac he would like to borrow it. At a second conference a few days later McClellan unexpectedly appeared. When asked about his plans he refused to answer. But he did say that in his own mind he had set a time for an advance.

A few days later he revealed to Lincoln what he intended to do. He would transport the troops under his command to the peninsula between the James and York rivers and then move overland upon Richmond. Lincoln, supported by the other generals whom he had consulted, preferred an overland advance from Washington following the route which McDowell, nine months earlier, had taken only to be balked at Bull Run. The President, inexperienced as he was in military matters, had grasped a fact which neither McClellan nor other Union commanders would comprehend: namely, that the Confederate Army rather than the Confederate capital was the true objective. McClellan would not yield nor would Lincoln, so an impasse kept the Army of

Lincoln and McClellan reach an impasse

the Potomac in its camps. On January 27, 1862, the President, without consulting any of his advisers, issued his General War Order No. 1. The order directed that on the twenty-second day of February, 1862, there would be a general movement of the land and naval forces of the United States against the Confederates, that the Army of the Potomac, the Army of West Virginia, the troops in Kentucky, the river flotilla at Cairo, and a naval force in the Gulf of Mexico be ready to move at that time, and that all commanders and their subordinates would be held to a prompt execution of the order.

The President orders a general advance

Four days later Lincoln issued Special War Order No. 1 to McClellan directing him, after providing for the defense of Washington, to form an expedition for occupying the point known as Manassas Junction and to be ready to move on or before the twenty-second day of February.

These orders elicited a long letter from the general emphasizing all the objections he could muster against a direct movement overland from Washington and insisting upon the plan of campaign which he had already advanced—transporting his army by water to the tip of the Peninsula and moving from that point northwest to Richmond.

Again the President and his principal general were stalemated. However, one Union commander was spoiling for a fight. Ulysses S. Grant, from his headquarters at Paducah, had looked covetously upon the two fortifications which protected the center of the Confederate line stretched across northern Tennessee and southern Kentucky. Fort Henry stood on the Tennessee River just south of the Kentucky border;

Joseph E. Johnston, fourth ranking officer
of the Confederate Army. He faced McClellan
at the beginning of the Peninsular Campaign.

*Simon Bolivar Buckner, C.S.A.
His superior officers made him
the goat at Fort Donelson.*

*Andrew H. Foote, U.S.N. His western
flotilla pounded Fort Henry into submission
on February 6, 1862. Wounded at Fort
Donelson on February 14, Foote died
four months later.*

Fort Donelson had been erected on the Cumberland River only twelve miles to the east. Grant was certain of success. He had an army of 15,000 and the aid of Commodore A. H. Foote's ironclad river gunboats, which the Navy Department had been building frantically since the preceding summer. General H. W. Halleck, now commanding the Department of the West, approved the movement and in early February the combined expedition started up the Tennessee River. Foote's guns opened on Fort Henry on February 6. The fortification, unfinished, was defended only by 117 artillerymen and surrendered after a short bombardment.

Grant, delayed by foul weather and almost impassable roads, arrived with his troops five days later. He marched at once to Fort Donelson and invested it on the twelfth. Unlike Henry, this would be no picnic. The fort, well-built, was garrisoned by 17,000 men. To add to Grant's troubles the weather, so far balmy, turned cold, and on the night of the thirteenth his men slept on frozen ground without shelters and all too often without blankets. Foote's gunboats arrived on the fourteenth but were repulsed by the guns of the fort. The next day the Confed-

70

Frying hardtack

erates left the protecting walls, attacked the surrounding Union troops, opened an escape route but failed to take advantage of it. Back again in Donelson they found themselves in a hopeless position. The two ranking generals, John B. Floyd and Gideon J. Pillow, who held their commands through political influence, abandoned the fort, leaving

Albert Sidney Johnston, second ranking officer of the Confederate Army. Killed at Shiloh, April 6, 1862.

NEW YORK HISTORICAL SOCIETY

the responsibility to the old professional, Simon Bolivar Buckner, who had once come to Grant's rescue with a loan when he was down and out. Buckner found himself faced with surrender or annihilation. When he asked for terms Grant replied: "No terms except unconditional and immediate surrender can be accepted. I propose to move immediately upon your works." Buckner had no choice but to accept. The message and the fall of the fort made Grant a national hero. Shortly afterward he was promoted to the rank of major general.

In war, exalted reputations can often be impermanent. So it was with the hero of Fort Donelson. In March, the Confederate War Department began a concentration of its forces, some 40,000 in number, at Corinth, Mississippi. Albert Sidney Johnston, a West Pointer whom Jefferson Davis esteemed above all others in the Southern armies, commanded in the West, charged with crushing Grant before he could be reinforced. The Union commander brought his

A, or wedge tents

own troops together at Pittsburg Landing on the Tennessee River, twenty-two miles northeast of Corinth. With curious neglect Grant gave no orders for entrenchments and had no plan of action in case of attack. He had no idea, he admitted later, that the Confederate Army would take the initiative. On the afternoon of April 5 he stated that "there will be no fight at Pittsburg Landing: we will have to go to Corinth."

Shortly before six o'clock on Sunday morning, April 6, while the Union troops were frying their bacon and boiling their coffee, the Confederates struck from the woods which had concealed their advance. The Union lines, thrown into confusion, gave ground. Grant, at Savannah, nine miles from the battlefield, heard the roar of guns and came up by steamboat. He sent couriers to Don Carlos Buell, commanding 20,000 men of the Army of the Ohio, and to Lew Wallace, with a division at Crump's Landing several miles distant, ordering them to bring up their troops as fast as possible. Before either relief column could arrive, thousands of fugitives were cowering under the bluffs along the river—white-faced, frightened men who by good luck had escaped death and had no heart to hazard their lives again.

In the middle of the afternoon Albert Sidney Johnston was killed and Beauregard, the second in command, took over. The Confederate Army had carried the day, but the new commander, unaware of the extent of the victory, gave orders to suspend the attack. That night both Buell and Wallace arrived with fresh men and took positions in the Union line. On the following morning Grant ordered an attack. The Confederate troops resisted stubbornly, but by nightfall were in full retreat toward Corinth.

Although a Union victory, Shiloh was costly. Out of 62,000 men, Grant lost 13,047, killed, wounded, or missing, while Johnston and Beauregard lost a quarter of their 40,000 troops. Although Grant would deny it to the end of his life, he had undoubtedly been caught unawares and had been fortunate to escape a major disaster.

Meanwhile in Washington, Lincoln, though with misgivings, had come to an agreement with McClellan. On condition that the general would leave Washington "entirely secure" the President authorized him to move the Army of the Potomac by water to the Peninsula and from there begin his advance upon Richmond. Before the general could put any of his troops on the transports, a naval battle in Hampton Roads threatened not only to thwart his campaign but also to panic every Northern city along the Atlantic coast.

Soon after the attack on Fort Sumter, the Union had abandoned the navy yard at Norfolk, Virginia, and destroyed the facilities and the ships which could not be taken to sea. Among these was the steamer *Merrimack,* which the commander had scuttled and burned to the

Water for the cook-house

72

Shiloh, April 6–7, 1862. The lithograph, though stylized, conveys a good impression of the terrain.

waterline. The Confederates raised the hull, built a superstructure, sheathed it with wrought iron plates and renamed the vessel *Virginia*. The ship was armed with two 7-inch guns and eight of smaller caliber. In addition she was equipped with a cast-iron prow with which she could ram opposing ships if she could get close enough. The *Virginia* was slow and unwieldy but she had lethal possibilities.

The Union Navy Department knew, at least in general, what the Confederates were doing with the *Merrimack* and set about to checkmate them. The Swedish-born naval architect and engineer, John Ericsson, came up with a novel design—a revolving turret housing two 11-inch guns and mounted on an armored raft-like deck. Essentially the craft would be a floating battery. Aware of the potential threat of the *Merrimack,* the shipyard at Greenpoint, Long Island, raced to complete Ericsson's naval innovation. The strange ship, christened the *Monitor,* was launched late in January, 1862, and turned over to the Federal government on February 19.

73

The battle of the Merrimack (Virginia) *and the* Monitor
in Hampton Roads, Virginia, March 9, 1862

On March 8 the *Virginia* steamed into Hampton Roads, where she found several wooden ships that were the pride of the Union Navy. She rammed the 30-gun *Cumberland,* which sank in a short time, and then forced the 50-gun *Congress* aground. After a heavy fire the ship surrendered. Three other Federal frigates ran aground while approaching the scene of battle. Late in the afternoon the *Virginia* retired with the intention of returning the next day to complete the destruction of the wooden ships.

Coming back the following morning, the *Virginia* found the *Monitor* lying next to the *Minnesota,* the *Virginia*'s intended victim. (Gideon Welles, the Union Secretary of the Navy, had anticipated the *Virginia*'s first move and had sent the *Monitor* down from New York on March 6.) For three hours the two ironclads exchanged shots. Neither could do substantial damage to the other although both scored many direct hits. Shortly after noon the *Virginia* sailed back to Norfolk and there remained for the next several weeks. It was obvious that she was too unseaworthy to be a threat to the Union Navy and the cities along the Atlantic coast. She had nevertheless demonstrated that no wooden ship could stand up to an ironclad and that all the navies of the world were outmoded.

With the *Virginia* no longer a menace, the passage from Washington to Fort Monroe at the tip of the Peninsula was safe. In mid-

*Officer's wall tent
with fly*

74

Thomas Jonathan ("Stonewall") Jackson. His campaign in the Shenandoah Valley in the spring of 1862 frightened the Lincoln administration.

March McClellan started to embark his troops on transports. By early April, with 100,000 men ashore, he began his advance toward Richmond, sixty-five miles to the northwest. Almost at once he encountered a Confederate force entrenched at Yorktown, where eighty-one years earlier Cornwallis had surrendered to Washington. Characteristically, McClellan overestimated the strength of his opponents and began a siege operation when one brisk assault would have dispersed the defenders. A month passed before he took the position and even then he allowed the Confederate troops to escape.

Before McClellan settled down in front of Yorktown, the Confederate authorities embarked upon a campaign which threw the Lincoln administration into consternation. Thomas Jonathan Jackson, the former Virginia Military Institute professor who had won the sobriquet of "Stonewall" at Bull Run, was given a small army with which to operate in the Shenandoah Valley. By rapid movements he convinced his Union adversaries that his strength was much greater than it was. Through sheer audacity he won victory after victory. Lincoln and the War Department, worried about the safety of the capital, withheld some 55,000 men who would otherwise have been sent to reinforce McClellan.

The hospital or wall tent

A thousand miles to the southwest the Federals fared better. New Orleans was not only a haven for blockade-runners but also the port through which the produce of the lower Mississippi Valley found its way to Europe to pay for badly needed Confederate imports. Its reduction was a prime objective for the Union. To capture the city and its defenses the Navy Department picked David Glasgow Farragut, a sixty-one-year-old native of Tennessee who had served in the Navy since he was nine years old. Farragut was given seventeen ships and a mortar flotilla, and transports accompanying the expedition carried 18,000 troops. Formidable defenses protected the Louisiana metropolis. On the Mississippi, forty miles above the Gulf, stood Fort Jackson on one side of the river and Fort St. Philip on the other. A defending flotilla lay above the forts. On April 18 Farragut's mortar flotilla, under Commander David D. Porter, began a bombardment of Fort Jackson which lasted for several days and nights without doing any considerable damage. Farragut, contrary to his orders and against the advice of his ablest officers, decided to "run" the forts—to steam straight past them to New Orleans. His ships were subjected to heavy fire but only three were sunk. The next day his fleet destroyed most of the Confederate flotilla. On the day after the battle Farragut took New Orleans without bloodshed and the Federal troops garrisoned the largest city in the South.

In Virginia, McClellan, having finally hurdled the Confederate barrier at Yorktown, pushed on toward Richmond. Joseph E. Johnston

The dog or shelter tent

*David G. Farragut, who commanded the Union fleet that
battered its way to New Orleans in April, 1862. Sixty-
one in 1862, he had served in the Navy since he was nine.*

pulled back his troops to favorable positions and called in Stonewall Jackson from the Shenandoah Valley. On May 31 Johnston tried to stop McClellan at Fair Oaks, only six miles from Richmond. Although the battle was a Union victory, McClellan did not take advantage of it. Johnston, severely wounded, gave up the Confederate command to Robert E. Lee, who, after an inglorious experience in western Virginia, had been serving as a kind of military adviser to the Confederate President.

Soon after Lee's appointment a series of engagements known as the "Seven Days Battles" took place, lasting from June 26 to July 2. The fortunes of the two armies varied in bloody fighting, the Confederates holding the advantage one day and the Federals the next. McClellan, always timorous, decided to pull back instead of risking all in a drive on Richmond. In the end, defeated in his own mind if not in fact, he changed his base from the York River to Harrison's Landing on the James, where he would be covered by the fire of Union gunboats. The change of base was a masterly maneuver, but the fact that it was a retreat could not be concealed. The Peninsular Campaign was over. Union casualties numbered 16,000 and Confederate losses were even larger. However, Richmond had been saved and the Union Army and

McClellan fails to take Richmond

its commander were too demoralized to take the offensive. From his headquarters McClellan blamed the Administration for his failure, going so far in insubordination as to declare to the Secretary of War: "If I save this army now, I tell you plainly that I owe no thanks to you or to any other persons in Washington. You have done your best to sacrifice this army." Lincoln, with all the tact he could muster, tried to mollify his commander. "If you think you are not strong enough to take Richmond just now, I do not ask you to try just now. Save the army, material, and personnel, and I will strengthen it for the offensive again as fast as I can."

Nevertheless, Lincoln found himself sorely tried by McClellan's complaints and recriminations. In his opinion the general had come to the end of his usefulness. The President turned to a Westerner, John Pope, whom he had known since boyhood. Pope, a Regular Army officer, had distinguished himself at Island No. 10, a fortified island in the Mississippi, fifty miles below Cairo. In March and April, 1862, the Union commander, in co-operation with Flag Officer Andrew H. Foote of the Navy, had landed a force and captured about half of the 12,000 Confederate defenders. To Lincoln, Pope seemed to have the aggressiveness that the Army of the Potomac needed.

Instead of replacing McClellan, Lincoln created a new army, the Army of Virginia, and put Pope at its head. The army was to consist of the Union forces in Virginia which had not been engaged on the Peninsula and of some of McClellan's troops as soon as they could be

David D. Porter. He commanded the mortar fleet under Farragut at New Orleans, and had charge of the Mississippi Squadron for two years after September, 1862.

Mortar boat

Robert E. Lee, third ranking officer in the Confederate Army, took over the defense of Richmond after Joseph E. Johnston was seriously wounded in the battle of Seven Pines, May 31, 1862. Lee had acquired his famous horse, "Traveller," earlier that spring.

brought back to Washington and sent to the new commander.

Soon after assuming command Pope made his first mistake. On July 14 he issued an address to his army. "I have come to you from the West," he announced, "where we have always seen the backs of our enemies; from an army whose business it has been to seek the adversary and to beat him when he was found; whose policy has been attack and not defense. . . . The strongest position a soldier should desire to occupy is one from which he can most easily advance against the enemy. Let us study the probable lines of retreat of our opponents, and leave our own to take care of themselves. Let us look before us, and not behind. Success and glory are in the advance, disaster and shame lurk in the rear." Officers and men, especially those who had served under McClellan, knew that they had fought well and resented Pope's slurs. The new commander's bombast destroyed whatever chance he had of winning the respect and confidence of the rank and file.

To bolster the eastern command further, Lincoln brought Henry W. Halleck from St. Louis to Washington. Known in the army as "Old

Camp barber

80

Brains," Halleck had graduated third in his West Point class of 1839, had written two books on the art of war, and had served in California during the Mexican War. He had resigned his commission in 1854 but at the outbreak of the Civil War had accepted an appointment as major general. In bringing him east, Lincoln expected him to serve as his military adviser and general in chief.

By the summer of 1862 Lincoln had become deeply impressed with the importance of slavery in the contest. In the beginning he had considered the object of the war to be the restoration of the Union, but as the months passed he had come to see that Negro slavery was a strong force in preventing the realization of that aim. Slaves working in the fields of the South produced crops that helped to feed the Confederate armies and thus released for active duty men who otherwise could not have been spared from the plantations. If slaves were given their freedom, it was probable that many thousands in gratitude would volunteer for service in the Union armies. Emancipation, moreover, would have a strong appeal to the liberal classes in England and in Europe and could very well prevent England and France from recognizing the Confederate government. Under the Constitution, only the states could emancipate slaves within their borders. To encourage them to do so Lincoln urged the loyal border states in which slavery existed to free their slaves in return for compensation by the Federal government. In the spring of 1862 he pleaded with repre-

Milk ration

General and Mrs. George B. McClellan. Had the general been more discreet in letters to his wife he might have gone down in history as a greater man.

81

Major General John Pope, who failed ingloriously at Second Bull Run

Major General Henry W. Halleck. Called to Washington from the West in 1862, and given the title of general in chief, he never succeeded in making himself more than Lincoln's military adviser.

sentatives from Delaware, Maryland, Kentucky, Missouri, and the new state of West Virginia to take this action. Indecisive and timorous, they failed to act on his recommendation. The only result of his effort was the abolition by Congress of slavery in the District of Columbia with compensation to the owners deprived of their property.

Lincoln decides to emancipate the slaves

Having failed to induce the border states to initiate emancipation, Lincoln decided to act himself under the extraordinary powers which he believed the Constitution gave the President in time of war. On July 22, 1862, at a meeting of his Cabinet, he read to the members the draft of a proclamation warning the states in rebellion that if they did not return to their allegiance by January 1, 1863, he would declare their slaves to be forever free. Lincoln told the members frankly that he had not called them together to ask their advice about the step which he proposed to take but that he would be glad to listen to whatever comments they had to make about phraseology. Secretary of State Seward, while approving the proclamation, questioned the timing. Recalling the recent succession of Union defeats, he thought that the measure would be considered the expedient of an exhausted government—"that it would be considered our last *shriek* on the retreat." Lincoln confessed later that Seward's objection struck him "with very great force." It was an aspect of the situation which he had overlooked. As a result he put the draft of the proclamation aside to wait

82

The charge across the "Burnside Bridge," a high point in the battle of Antietam, September 17, 1862. Sketch by Edwin Forbes, special artist for Leslie's.

for the victory which he hoped the new commander of the Army of Virginia would give him.

Pope planned to concentrate his scattered forces at Culpeper on the Orange and Alexandria Railroad some fifty miles southwest of Washington. Lee, with Richmond safe, decided to test the new Federal commander. As a first move he sent Stonewall Jackson to strike at the Union force under Nathaniel P. Banks before Banks could reach the point of concentration. Banks, overconfident, attacked Jackson at Cedar Mountain, ten miles south of Culpeper, on August 9. Banks did not know that Jackson had been heavily reinforced and could bring into battle twice the number of men in his own command. The result was a sharp Union defeat.

Four-wheeled ambulance

Lee now moved to strike Pope's main army before more of McClellan's troops could join it. Dividing his army—a daring maneuver—the Confederate commander sent Jackson and J. E. B. Stuart around Pope's right flank to destroy the Federal supply depot at Manassas Junction. The movement succeeded. Pope, now thoroughly frightened by an enemy army between him and Washington, began to withdraw toward the capital. An abler general, and one less confused, might have struck Lee's army while divided and crushed it piecemeal.

*A part of Lee's army crossing the Potomac in the invasion of
Maryland, September 15, 1862. Sketch by Alfred R. Waud.*

Pope missed the opportunity. Lee succeeded in bringing his scattered
forces together at Manassas on August 29. Two days of confused and
severe fighting ensued. Pope, soundly defeated, retreated. On September 1 Lee struck the rear guard of the Army of Virginia near
Chantilly and inflicted severe punishment. Knowing that heavy reinforcements were on their way to Pope, the Confederate leader gave up
the pursuit. In this second battle of Manassas, Pope had lost 16,000
men to Lee's loss of 9000. "The outcome," one authority has remarked,
"pointed up the marked superiority of Southern generalship at this
stage of the war in the East."

Pope's incapacity was thrown into relief by the bombast which
preceded it and by the whining recriminations he permitted himself.
Lincoln, disillusioned, merged the Army of Virginia with the Army of
the Potomac and reluctantly restored McClellan to command.

Lee, ever audacious, decided to take advantage of the Federal

84

demoralization and confusion and invade the North. By his own statement he hoped to tap the fertile farms of Maryland for food and forage,
and to swing the people of that commonwealth to the active support
of the Confederacy. He also counted on inflicting another punishing
defeat on the Army of the Potomac before winter set in. On September
4 the Army of Northern Virginia began to cross the Potomac into
Maryland. There the citizens on whose sympathies Lee had counted
gave his men a cool welcome, but he pushed on. On September 14 at
South Mountain in the Blue Ridge chain twenty miles below the Pennsylvania border, the Union forces inflicted a sharp but not decisive
defeat on parts of Lee's army. McClellan, by an almost unbelievable
piece of good luck, found papers disclosing Lee's battle plan, but failed
to exploit the discovery promptly. On September 17 the two armies
faced each other on both sides of Antietam Creek near the little town
of Sharpsburg, Maryland. The battle which followed has been called
"the bloodiest single day of the war." Both armies suffered heavy
losses—the Federals 12,410 in killed, wounded, and missing out of
75,000, the Confederates 13,724 out of 52,000. Neither side could
claim a victory, but Lee's advance had been stopped. The next day
he ordered his army back to Virginia.

Drafting

Five days after the battle of Antietam, Lincoln called a cabinet meeting. As soon as all the members had arrived, the President read a
short chapter from a new book by Artemus Ward, then a popular
humorist. He enjoyed the reading. All the cabinet members smiled
dutifully except Stanton who made it obvious that he considered such
levity out of place. After the reading the President reminded those
present that two months earlier he had brought up the subject of
emancipation but had deferred action until the Union Army won a
major victory. He admitted that the outcome of Antietam was not as
decisive as he would have liked, but the Confederates had been driven
out of Maryland, and Pennsylvania no longer stood in danger of
invasion. "When the rebel army was at Frederick," he continued, "I
determined, as soon as it should be driven out of Maryland, to issue a
proclamation of emancipation, such as I thought most likely to be
useful. I said nothing to anyone, but I made the promise to myself and
to my Maker. The rebel army is now driven out, and I am going to
fulfill that promise."

Company cook

Lincoln reiterated his July assertion that he had decided to issue the
proclamation and asked only for suggestions as to its wording or other
minor features. All the cabinet members agreed that emancipation was
a necessity, although Montgomery Blair, the Postmaster General,
expressed the fear that it would have a bad effect upon the border
states and on the army. Seward made a suggestion or two which
Lincoln readily accepted. That afternoon the President signed the

Lincoln at McClellan's headquarters at Antietam after the battle.
McClellan stands fourth on the left of the President. This is one
of the best of Alexander Gardner's photographs of the Civil War.

engrossed copy and on the following day it was published in full by the leading newspapers of the country.

McClellan devoted the first weeks after the battle of Antietam to resting and equipping the Army of the Potomac. He also reverted to form and demanded heavy reinforcements. Two weeks after the battle he reported that the army was not in condition to undertake a campaign and that he intended to do no more than wait and attack the enemy should he again attempt an invasion of Maryland. Lincoln, dismayed, made a visit to McClellan in an attempt to impress upon him the necessity of action. McClellan listened but made no promises. On October 6, after Lincoln's return to Washington, Halleck, as general in chief, ordered McClellan to cross the Potomac and give battle to the enemy. McClellan paid no attention and complained that the army could not move because it was deficient in all manner of supplies. Finally, when it became evident that the Union commander had no intention of undertaking a campaign in the foreseeable future, Lincoln ordered him to turn over the command to General Ambrose E. Burnside.

The thirty-eight-year-old Burnside, who looked older than his years because of the distinctive side whiskers he affected, had graduated from the United States Military Academy in 1847. After spending six

Dismounted

86

years in the Army he had resigned to establish a manufacturing business. When that failed he had entered the Land Department of the Illinois Central Railroad, a position which McClellan had obtained for him.

At the outbreak of the war Burnside had organized the 1st Rhode Island Regiment. He had handled his men well in the first battle of Bull Run and had served creditably in coastal operations in the early months of 1862. In the spring of that year he had been promoted to the rank of major general.

Burnside had twice declined the command of the Army of the Potomac. He knew himself to be a competent corps commander, but he did not believe that he could handle a large army. However, from the beginning of the war he had made a strong and favorable impression upon Lincoln. Now the President saw him as the best man available. Burnside, well aware that he was expected to take the offensive as soon as possible, proposed to move his army to Fredericksburg, Virginia, cross the Rappahannock, seize the heights south of the town, and then strike for Richmond. Lincoln approved this plan reluctantly. He would have preferred that Burnside make Lee's army rather than the capital of the Confederacy his objective, but he was unwilling to overrule his new general at the outset of his command.

Bad planning, bad execution, and bad luck bedeviled Burnside's campaign from the beginning. The most critical misadventure was the failure of the War Department to supply promptly the pontoons which Burnside needed for crossing the Rappahannock. By December 10, when the pontoons had come and the Union commander began the perilous crossing, Lee had brought his army together and had occupied the heights at Fredericksburg in strong positions north and south of that town. On December 13 Burnside sent his troops forward in a series of unrelated frontal attacks against strong positions which Lee parried by shifting brigades of his smaller army to reinforce his lines where they were threatened. It was on this occasion that the Confederate commander, watching Burnside's troops advance to destruction, exclaimed: "It is well that war is so terrible! We should grow too fond of it!" Never had the Army of the Potomac displayed more valor, never had it suffered more grievously or to smaller purpose. When the battle ended with early winter nightfall, nearly 1300 Union soldiers lay piled in rows while thousands of wounded suffered through the cold night hoping, often in vain, to be picked up by the stretcher bearers. Confederate losses in killed, wounded, and missing were less than half of those of the Union. The Army of the Potomac would never undergo a more humiliating defeat.

Fredericksburg: a Union disaster

For the disaster Burnside, a man of candor and integrity, took full responsibility. After the disaster he wrote to Halleck: "The fact that

The Cabinet considering the Emancipation Proclamation. Reproduced here is an engraving, by A. H. Ritchie, made from the painting by Francis B. Carpenter. For the scene, Carpenter relied on statements by Lincoln and cabinet members.

The Baltimore satirist Volck took a different view of the writing of the Emancipation Proclamation.

I decided to move . . . on this line, rather against the opinion of the President, Secretary of War, and yourself, and that you left the whole movement in my hands without giving me orders, makes me responsible."

Too readily one thinks of the Civil War in terms of the big battles—Fredericksburg, Antietam, the Peninsula, first and second Bull Run. Yet some of the smaller battles involved a sufficient number of men and resulted in casualties heavy enough to have been considered major engagements in the first months of the war. At Munfordville, Kentucky, on the same days that Lee and McClellan were engaged at Antietam, the Confederate General Braxton Bragg captured more than 4000 Union troops together with large stores and 5000 stand of small arms. On September 19, at Iuka, Mississippi, two Union divisions under William S. Rosecrans and a Confederate force commanded by Sterling Price tangled in a sharp engagement in which Union forces lost 790 men and the Confederates twice that number. In the first week of October, Rosecrans and the Confederate Van Dorn fought for the possession of Corinth, Mississippi, a battle in which 44,000 men were engaged and in which losses totaled more than 5000. Only days later at Perryville, Kentucky, Don Carlos Buell, at the head of the Union Army of the Ohio, struck Bragg's 16,000 men with a much larger force and just missed achieving a significant victory. The little town of Prairie Grove in faraway Arkansas saw a sharp battle between Federal and Confederate forces, each numbering 10,000, on December 7. At Holly Springs, Mississippi, on December 20, Van Dorn caught a Federal force off guard and destroyed supplies essential to the campaign which Grant had already mounted against Vicksburg.

The turkey he didn't catch

Almost daily over the country men died in skirmishes and encounters too small to be recorded by anyone except the most pedantic chronicler. And for every man who died from a gunshot wound, several gave their lives to the diseases endemic in both armies—dysentery, typhoid fever, and pneumonia.

Even when one adds the small engagements to the big battles he does not tell the whole story of the war. Much of every soldier's life was sheer boredom—killing time in camp when the rains turned the roads into impassable morasses, or marching ten miles this day and fifteen the next only to find that the sought-for enemy had slipped away, or had never existed in anything more real than the volatile imaginations of a handful of cavalrymen. And which was worse—the sluggish hours in camp or the fruitless marching—was a toss-up.

Drumming out of camp

Boredom on land was matched by boredom at sea. In the wastes of the Atlantic, often gray and storm-tossed, and in the warmer waters of the Gulf of Mexico, seamen spent days on end without sighting a sail. Yet throughout 1862 the Union blockade became steadily more effective. By December the Federal Navy had 427 ships in commission, almost twice the number with which it had started the year. On the other hand blockade-runners became more numerous and more efficient. Ships—low, sleek and fast—were built specially to evade or run from the Union patrols. Blockade-running meant high risks but enormous profits. The runners turned increasingly to the luxuries which occupied little space in the holds and brought the biggest returns. The importation of the heavy goods—guns, ammunition, powder, and salt—which the Confederacy so badly needed, suffered. Gideon Welles exaggerated only slightly when he stated on December 1, 1862, "that in no previous war had the ports of an enemy's country been so effectually closed by a naval force."

The Confederacy found a way of striking back. Its naval agent in England, Captain James D. Bulloch, contracted for several commerce raiders to be built by private shipyards. The first of these, the *Alabama*, slipped out to sea on May 15, 1862, through the negligence of British authorities. In the Azores she was fitted with guns and ammunition and took on coal and a very able commander, Captain Raphael Semmes. For more than two years she cruised the Atlantic sinking,

Ambrose E. Burnside, Commander of the Army of the Potomac, November, 1862, to January, 1863. He knew that he was not equal to the job.

Marye's Heights, Fredericksburg. Federal forces fought bravely, vainly, and with exorbitant cost to take this position.

burning or capturing sixty-nine ships. The *Florida,* a second raider, managed to put to sea during the year to be outfitted at Nassau. Under a daring commander, John Newland Maffitt, the *Florida* in her two-year career captured or destroyed thirty-seven U.S. ships.

In the last week of the year guns blazed as violently as they had in April and June and September. In one of his many preliminary moves against Vicksburg, Grant sent Sherman with 32,000 men to take the Chickasaw Bluffs, a few miles north of the Mississippi city. The Confederates occupied a strong position. Sherman made his first attack on December 29, but his men were stopped at the base of the bluff. A few days later the Union commander, whose forces had lost 1776 men, gave up the attack.

Four hundred miles to the northeast a bigger, bloodier battle swirled as the year ended. On December 30 Rosecrans' Army of the Cumberland and the Confederate Army of Tennessee under Braxton Bragg faced each other at Stones River near the town of Murfreesboro in north central Tennessee. Each commander intended to attack the other, and each planned to strike the opposing right flank. As dawn broke on the thirty-first, Bragg hit hard. At first Rosecrans did not realize the force of the blow and continued with his own plans. He soon saw the necessity of shifting his forces to bolster his own lines instead of taking the offensive. Bragg threw one division after another

Fall in for roll-call

91

Major General William S. Rosecrans. At the end of the year, in command of the Army of the Cumberland, he fought Bragg to a draw at Stones River.

against the Union lines. Sheridan, holding a narrow front, put up a stubborn resistance although he was forced to pull back.

The savage fighting lasted all day with Rosecrans showing the highest qualities of generalship, continually strengthening and reforming his lines. With the early winter twilight the action tapered off. At the close of the day Bragg sent an exultant dispatch to Richmond. "The enemy has yielded his strong point and is falling back. We occupy the whole field and shall follow. . . . God has granted us a happy new year."

The Confederate commander boasted prematurely. Rosecrans had retreated, but only to take up stronger positions. At the conclusion of the day's battle he had decided to await an enemy's attack and to order up fresh supplies of ammunition. On January 1 Bragg realized that the Union forces were going to stand and fight. He also learned the extent of his losses the day before. With both antagonists wary, the first day of 1863 passed in quiet.

On January 2 Bragg ordered Breckinridge to strike the Union line with his full force. For a short time it looked as if he would break it, but artillery changed the tide of battle and inflicted heavy punishment upon the attackers. That night rain fell and the plowed fields became quagmires. Rain fell again the next day and both commanders saw that continuation of the battle was impossible. Quietly Bragg drew back his army. With the roads very nearly impassable Rosecrans decided against pursuit. Bragg claimed a tactical victory but one not worth the cost. Rosecrans deserved the telegram he received from Lincoln: "God bless you and all with you! Please tender to all, and accept for yourself the nation's gratitude for your and their skill, endurance, and dauntless courage."

The Monitor's *sturdy performance against the* Merrimack *was only one evidence that Gideon Welles, U.S. Secretary of the Navy, was building a formidable fighting force.*

In the Navy Department, Welles was ably abetted by his First Assistant Secretary, Gustavus Vasa Fox, a former naval officer.

The Confederate ironclad Merrimack (Virginia) *sinking the wooden* Cumberland *in Hampton Roads on March 8, 1862. From an engraving after a painting by J. O. Davidson.*

An episode in the battle of Elkhorn Tavern, or Pea
Ridge, March 7–8, 1862. The artist, self-taught, was
a Confederate sergeant, Hunt P. Wilson.

At Elkhorn Tavern in northwestern Arkansas, a strong Confederate force under Earl Van Dorn attacked a Union army commanded by Samuel Curtis. Another phase of the action as Sergeant Hunt saw it.

Sketch, by Alfred R. Waud, of a fight at Occoquan, Virginia, on January 28, 1862. One of the thousands of small engagements remembered only by close students of the war.

Alfred R. Waud sketched a Federal charge at Kernstown, Virginia, on March 23, 1862—one of the first engagements of Stonewall Jackson's Valley Campaign. At Kernstown, Jackson met with a rare repulse.

Camp Douglas, Chicago. This prison camp was set up to take care of Confederates captured at Forts Henry and Donelson, February, 1862.

These men fought under Jackson in the Valley Campaign. From a water color by W. L. Sheppard.

Site of the battle of Shiloh. On tangled, desolate terrain like this the two armies lost nearly 24,000 men (killed, wounded, and missing) in two days. A postwar photo.

An artist's conception of the fighting at Shiloh. Grant, on horseback, is pictured near the right margin.

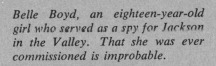

Belle Boyd, an eighteen-year-old
girl who served as a spy for Jackson
in the Valley. That she was ever
commissioned is improbable.

Louis Philippe Albert d'Orleans,
Comte de Paris, and Robert
Philippe Louis Eugène Ferdinand
d'Orleans, Comte de Chartres—
French royal princes who served on
McClellan's staff.

The 1st Connecticut Heavy Artillery in 1862. The battery was commanded by Colonel Robert O. Tyler, in charge of the siege batteries. Officers and men show far more "spit and polish" than they would a year or two later.

From this primitive church the bloody battle of Shiloh, April 6–7, 1862, took its name. The Confederates called it Pittsburg Landing.

To reduce Yorktown, McClellan undertook a formal siege. Shown here is a mortar battery, firing heavy projectiles in a high, arching trajectory.

Federal troops in peaceful Yorktown, where the British forces had surrendered at the end of the Revolutionary War, held McClellan in check from April 5 to May 4 at the outset of the Peninsular Campaign.

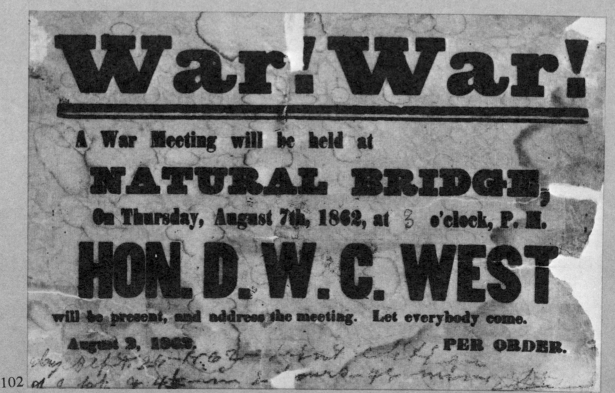

Left poster text:

RECRUITS WANTED!

"Time is Everything."

Having been authorized by

GOV. YATES

To raise a Company of men, for three years or during the war, I have opened an Office in the building lately occupied by Mr. R. Bills,

On Hamilton St., adjoining 'Peoria House,' for the purpose of recruiting said company.

Forty Dollars Cash

paid on being mustered into the U.S. Service.

Dont wait until DRAFTING commences but come up like MEN, and show your PATRIOTISM by enlisting and helping with all your power to restore again to its once proud position, that

GLORIOUS OLD FLAG!

The STARS AND STRIPES.

PEORIA, July 19th, 1862.

M. V. HOTCHKISS.

R. Foster, Printer and Bookbinder, Peoria.

Right poster text:

RALLY! PEOPLE

of Montgomery, Chester & Delaware Counties.

AWAKE!   SPIRITS OF '76.

A GRAND

WAR MEETING!

Of the People will be held at the Grove of Charles Arthur, Esq.

ON LANCASTER PIKE,

Above the 9 Mile Stone,

ON THURSDAY AFTERNOON, AUG. 7,

At Half-Past Two O'clock,

Come as comes the tempest rushing,   From each rocky hill and valley,
Bending forests in its path,   Sweep away the invading band.
As the mountain torrent gushing,   In the name of Freedom rally,
As the billows in their wrath;   To defend your Native Land!

Merchants, Mechanics, Farmers and Laboring Men, Rally! Come from your Counting Rooms, your Workshops, and your Fields, and show by your presence your devotion to your country.

The following champions of the Union will address the Meeting:

Hon. Isaac Hazelhurst, Thos. S. Darling, Esq., Horatio Gates Jones, Esq., Rev. J. W. Jackson, George Northrop, Esq., G. G. Rakestraw, Esq., Rev. J. P. Heck and Judge Kelley.

The INDEPENDENT BRASS BAND of Manayunk

WILL BE IN ATTENDANCE.

The North responded to the failure of McClellan's campaign on the Peninsula with stiffened resolution. At Peoria, Illinois, recruits were offered $40 for enlisting.

The residents of southeastern Pennsylvania were summoned to a war rally. "In the name of Freedom rally, To defend your Native Land!"

The South also held its rallies, as this poster summoning the people to a war meeting at Natural Bridge, Virginia, proves. Few Southern broadsides of this kind have survived.

Bottom poster text:

War! War!

A War Meeting will be held at

NATURAL BRIDGE,

On Thursday, August 7th, 1862, at 3 o'clock, P. M.

HON. D. W. C. WEST

will be present, and address the meeting. Let everybody come.

August 3, 1862.   PER ORDER.

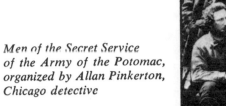

Men of the Secret Service of the Army of the Potomac, organized by Allan Pinkerton, Chicago detective

Another group of Pinkerton's men. Their inaccurate reports led McClellan consistently to overestimate the numbers and strength of his opponents.

Yorktown after the Confederates withdrew. It was the first Southern city to be battered into rubble by Union guns.

McClellan used aerial reconnaissance throughout the Peninsular Campaign. An unidentified artist painted T. S. C. Lowe's "balloon wagon."

Servants of the French princes at Yorktown

Review of Union troops at Cumberland Landing on the Pamunkey River in the early weeks of the Peninsular Campaign. Note the blacksmith's anvil at the lower right of the photograph.

105

Bridging the Chickahominy, June, 1862

*Lowe, the balloonist,
making an ascension
at Fair Oaks,
Virginia, June, 1862.*

The Confederate cavalryman, Nathan Bedford Forrest, a former slave dealer, saw his reputation grow in 1862.

Brigadier General J. E. B. Stuart, C.S.A. His star rose when he rode around McClellan's army in June, 1862.

Brigadier General Turner Ashby, C.S.A., photographed in death. His star set when he was killed at Harrisonburg, Virginia, on June 6, 1862.

107

Volck, not always satirical, showed smugglers bringing medicines into the South, hard-pressed for drugs.

The South was equally hard-pressed for metal to be cast into guns and shells. In Volck's drawing, church bells are being offered to the foundries.

At New Orleans, General Ben Butler, commanding the occupying troops, made himself hated throughout the South. A. J. Volck sketched Butler's civilian "victims" at Fort St. Philip, on the Mississippi below the city.

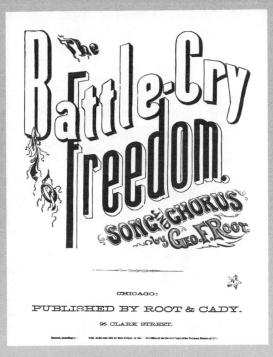

The South had a new song:
"The despot's heel is on thy shore,
Maryland! My Maryland!"
But Maryland failed to respond.

A Northern response to Lincoln's call for troops in July, 1862:

"We are coming, coming, coming,
We are coming, coming, coming,
We are coming, coming, coming,
Father Abraham,
Three hundred thousand more."

Patriotic fervor in the summer of 1862 gave birth to one of the great war songs of the Union. A rally in Chicago heard the refrain:

"We'll rally round the flag, boys, we'll rally once again,
Shouting the Battle Cry of Freedom!"

before the song was published.

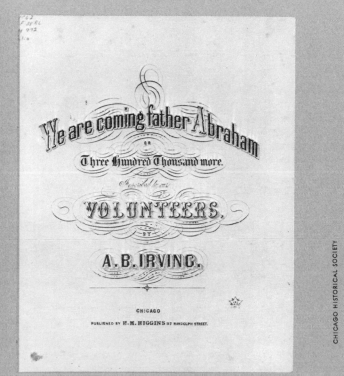

PROCLAMATION.

To the Inhabitants of Kentucky!

Fellow Countrymen--

I HAVE KEPT MY PROMISE.

At the head of my old companions in arms, I am once more amongst you, with God's blessing no more to leave you.

Deprived as you are by these Northern Despots of all true information respecting the War, you are probably unaware that our holy Southern cause is everywhere in the ascendant.

The so-called "Young Napoleon," McClellan, has retreated from the Peninsula. Stonewall Jackson, the 'invincible,' is asserting the superiority of our Southern Banner against the armies of Pope, Banks, Fremont, Burnside, and that of McClellan, who has joined them. His ultimate success is assured.

NO POWER ON EARTH CAN MAKE US SLAVES!

Bragg, in Tennessee, is steadily advancing with an overwhelming force on Buel, who is retreating, whilst New Orleans is on the eve of being torn from the clutches of "Butler, the infamous," and restored to its legitimate and Confederate Government.

Kirby Smith at the head of a powerful army, is already in your State, whilst Forrest, Woodward, and myself have already proven to the Yankees our existence by taking Murfreesboro, Gallatin and Clarksville, burning the railroad bridges and damaging seriously the enemy.

AROUSE, KENTUCKIANS! shake off that listless feeling which was engendered by the presence of a powerful and relentless enemy. He is no longer to be feared! We have drawn his eye-teeth! there will soon be nothing left of him but his roar!

Let the old men of Kentucky, and our noble-hearted women, arm their sons and their lovers for the fight! Better death in our sacred cause than a life of slavery!

Young men of Kentucky flock to my standard, it will always wave in the path of honor and history will relate how you responded to my appeal, and how, by so doing, you saved your country!

JOHN H. MORGAN,

Aug. 22 1862 Col.-Commanding Brigade, C. S. A.

[MORGAN'S PRESS PRINT.]

In this proclamation a flamboyant Confederate cavalryman appealed to his fellow Kentuckians to flock to his standard. "Better death in our sacred cause than a life of slavery!"

Captain Raphael Semmes, C.S.N. In 1862 he took command of the commerce raider Alabama, *and began the long cruise on which he would capture or destroy sixty-nine Union merchantmen.*

The Stone Bridge at Antietam, September 17, one of the focal points of the battle

Manassas Junction after the second battle of Bull Run

The human consequence of Petersburg battle

Rolling stock at Manassas while in Federal hands

A Confederate limber chest and dead artillerymen at Antietam

Some of the 2700 Confederates killed at Antietam

Fredericksburg, Virginia, during Burnside's attack

A group of slaves in 1862. In time, if not immediately, the Emancipation Proclamation would make them free.

Surgeon A. Hurd of the 14th Indiana Volunteers attending Confederate wounded at Antietam

Aquia Creek, on the Potomac near Fredericksburg. One of Burnside's supply points.

On these pontoon bridges, and three others, Burnside's troops crossed the Rappahannock preparatory to attacking Lee's army in and around Fredericksburg.

CHICAGO HISTORICAL SOCIETY

Belle Plain, Virginia, on the Potomac. Another of Burnside's supply points.

CHICAGO HISTORICAL SOCIETY

A telegraph operator at Fredericks-burg as sketched by Alfred R. Waud

*The telegraph in use at Fredericksburg.
Another Waud sketch.*

After crossing the Rappahannock at Fredericksburg, Federal troops found abandoned Confederate camps.

Fredericksburg, pounded to pieces without result by Union guns

Other Union casualties at Fredericksburg

*Incidents of the war.
Winslow Homer's rendering
of a malingerer.*

Repeated attacks at the base of Marye's Heights at Fredericksburg had no other result than this grim harvest.

The war had its lighter moments. Frank Vizetelly sketched an evening's entertainment in a Confederate camp near the end of 1862.

By the end of 1862 bounties had gone up. A Pennsylvania cavalry troop offered recruits $162 upon enlistment.

Another Pennsylvania regiment went a little higher, to $165.

Thirty-two-pound gun on the C.S.S. Teaser, a former tug converted into a gunboat. The Teaser was captured on July 4, 1862, in the James River.

A Union battery in 1862. Horses outnumbered men.

A feature of the war: the sutler, who sold luxuries and articles not issued by the quartermaster to the soldiers. The sutler, unpopular but indispensable, was robbed at every opportunity.

Libby Prison, a former warehouse in Richmond, housed captured Union officers. In notoriety it was second only to Andersonville.

Battery D, 5th U.S. Artillery (Regular Army), on the firing line. This picture is about as close to an action shot as the Civil War photographers, with their slow lenses, ever came.

Stones River, December 31, 1862–January 2, 1863. A participant made this stylized sketch of the charge of Beatty's Union brigade on December 31.

Union steamboats at Chickasaw Bluffs, north of Vicksburg, where Sherman was repulsed in the last week of December, 1862

121

A. E. Mathews of the 81st Ohio Volunteer Infantry,
pictured a lull in the fighting at Stones River.

Mathews sketched the charge of M. B. Walker's
Union Brigade on January 2, 1863.

THE YEAR
OF BIG BATTLES

WHILE the Union and Confederate armies, both sorely hurt, faced each other at Stones River on the first day of January, an event far more important than the lull in a great battle took place in Washington. There in the White House the annual New Year's reception began at eleven o'clock in the morning. Until two in the afternoon the President remained in the Blue Room greeting his guests. Quietly he slipped away to the Executive Office where he massaged his right hand so that he could hold a pen: he was about to sign an epoch-making document and he wanted his signature to show no evidence of indecision. He had asked no one to witness the event, but a dozen officials looked over his shoulder as he wrote in a firm hand his full name on the Proclamation of Emancipation. As soon as he had signed, the document was carried to the Department of State to be attested by the great seal and deposited in the archives of the government. News of the signing was immediately published to the world.

In its camps north of the Rappahannock, the Army of the Potomac smarted under its disastrous defeat at Fredericksburg. Burnside determined to retrieve his losses. On January 20 he began a forward movement. That same night a two-day rainstorm set in, small streams became impassable, and the surface of the roads turned into mud so deep that artillerymen had to struggle with the wheels of gun carriages

The Emancipation Proclamation, January 1, 1863. This facsimile, with embellishments, was sold at the Northwestern Sanitary Fair in Chicago, 1865, for the benefit of the Soldiers' Home. The original document was destroyed in the Chicago Fire, 1871.

to get them out of the mire. Under such conditions no action of any kind was possible. Although Burnside could not be held responsible for an act of God, the misfortune demonstrated that his usefulness was at an end. On January 25 General Joseph Hooker took command of the Army of the Potomac.

The new general, forty-nine years old, was a graduate of West Point and a veteran of the Seminole and Mexican Wars who had served in the Regular Army until 1853. Upon the outbreak of the Civil War he had been commissioned a brigadier general and had fought with distinction on the Peninsula and at Antietam and Fredericksburg. He had a reputation for loose living, loose talk, and insubordination, but his bravery and aggressive spirit were beyond question. In Lincoln's opinion, these qualities outweighed his defects.

Hooker began at once to restore the army to fighting trim. He called back men and officers on furlough and offered inducements to those absent without leave to return to the ranks. He saw that the men were better fed and that worn-out equipment was replaced. Every effort was made to restore discipline and to raise the morale of the troops from the low level to which it had sunk. As the days lengthened with the coming of spring and the grass in the fields turned green, the spirits of the army rose. The men knew that as soon as the roads were dry the new campaign would begin. After months of inactivity they looked forward to it.

Hooker planned carefully. Lee's army still occupied its defensive position overlooking Fredericksburg. Hooker knew from Burnside's disastrous experience that a frontal attack would be fatal. Instead he planned a wide sweep around Lee's left flank, leaving a third of his army to cross the Rappahannock and hold Lee in his entrenchments. The Confederate commander, with 60,000 men as compared with Hooker's 134,000, would be in danger of annihilation if the Union movements succeeded.

THE UNIONIST.

The battle began on May 1. Lee, with characteristic audacity, divided his army and attacked Hooker's advancing force. The Union commander, having heard reports that Lee had been heavily reinforced, faltered and the day's fighting ended inconclusively.

That night Lee and Stonewall Jackson decided upon a bold movement. Having found a guide who knew the way through the tangled wilderness, Lee sent Jackson with 26,000 men across the Federal front only two or three miles away to strike Hooker's exposed right flank. The movement succeeded and the Union forces were unaware that a good-sized army had marched sixteen miles without discovery. As twilight set in, Jackson's men struck General O. O. Howard's XI Corps on the extreme left of the Federal line. Howard's men broke in confusion. Except for the falling night and an agonizing Confederate

FREEDOM TO SLAVES!

Whereas, the President of the United States did, on the first day of the present month, issue his *Proclamation* declaring "that *all persons held as Slaves in certain designated States, and parts of States, are, and henceforward shall be free,*" and that the Executive Government of the United States, including the Military and Naval authorities thereof, would recognize and maintain the freedom of said persons. *And Whereas,* the county of *Frederick* is included in the territory designated by the Proclamation of the President, in which the *Slaves should become free,* I therefore hereby notify the citizens of the city of Winchester, and of said County, of said Proclamation, and of my intention to maintain and enforce the same.

I expect all citizens to yield a ready compliance with the Proclamation of the Chief Executive, and I admonish all persons disposed to resist its peaceful enforcement, that upon manifesting such disposition by acts, they will be regarded as rebels in arms against the lawful authority of the Federal Government and dealt with accordingly.

All persons liberated by said Proclamation are admonished to abstain from all violence, and immediately betake themselves to useful occupations.

The officers of this command are admonished and ordered to act in accordance with said proclamation and to yield their ready co-operation in its enforcement.

R. H. Milroy,
Brig. Gen'l Commanding.

Winchester Va.
Jan. 5th, 1863.

A Union commander gave notice of the Proclamation of Emancipation to the citizens of Winchester, Virginia.

The Southern sympathizer Volck saw prostitution and degradation as the result of the freeing of the slaves.

misfortune, a complete rout would have followed. The misfortune came when Jackson, riding ahead of his attacking line, was fired on by his own men and so severely wounded that he died a few days later.

On May 3 the battle resumed. Hooker, temporarily disabled by the concussion of a shell that struck near him, appeared to be hopelessly confused. Even on this third day of fighting, the Union Army was not defeated and might have turned Chancellorsville into a victory had it been skillfully handled. Hooker, however, never succeeded in bringing more than a part of his troops into action at any one time and at the end of the day concluded that there was no chance of success. Once again a much stronger Army of the Potomac had been vanquished by a smaller force under a superior general.

Chancellorsville: another defeat for the Army of the Potomac

Before 1862 had come to an end Grant, commanding in the West, had embarked on a campaign to open the Mississippi River and divide the Confederacy into two parts. The key to the situation was the heavily fortified city of Vicksburg, dominating the Mississippi from the high bluffs on which it was situated. The destruction of Grant's supply base at Holly Springs on December 20 and Sherman's repulse at Chickasaw Bluffs in the last week of the year were hardly an auspicious beginning.

In this impasse the Union commander turned to novel expedients. With the co-operation of Admiral David D. Porter, who commanded the Union River Fleet, he made five different attempts to bypass Vicksburg by cutting canals or changing river courses. All failed.

In April, 1863, Grant put his final plan into operation. He would march his troops through Louisiana on the west side of the Mississippi beyond the range of Vicksburg's guns to a point below the city where a crossing could be made. Porter would run his transports straight past Vicksburg's batteries, rendezvous with the army, and ferry the troops to the east side of the river. On the night of April 16 Porter sent twelve transports through the shot and shell of the Confederate batteries and lost only one. A few nights later six transports and thirteen barges repeated the attempt and while one transport and seven barges were lost, Grant now had sufficient shipping for his purpose.

While Grant was still west of the river he sent Benjamin H. Grierson, a cavalry commander who had formerly been a music teacher, on a daring raid to confuse and distract the Confederate forces in Tennessee and Mississippi. Grierson left La Grange, Tennessee, on April 17 with 1700 men. Sixteen days later he rode into the Union lines at Baton Rouge, Louisiana. He had destroyed many miles of railroad and 3000 stand of arms. He had taken 500 prisoners and escaped thousands of troops sent against him. The raid was one of the most successful cavalry operations of the entire war.

Grant and his men crossed to the east bank of the Mississippi on

Posted

127

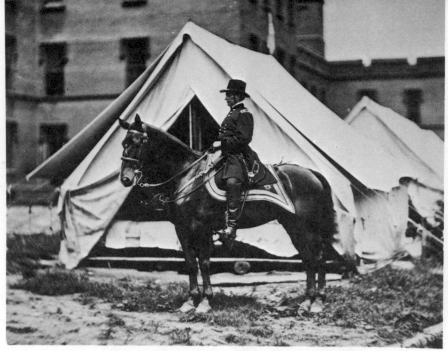

Major General Joseph Hooker, given command of the Army of the Potomac January 25, 1863

April 30. A week later, with 44,000 men, he moved on Jackson, Mississippi, the capital of the state. The defenders, 6000 in number, were defeated in a short but sharp battle.

Grant now turned west to attack Vicksburg from the rear. At Champion's Hill, halfway between Jackson and Vicksburg, a part of the Union army under McPherson and McClernand attacked and defeated John C. Pemberton, the Confederate commander charged with the defense of Vicksburg. Pemberton made a stand the next day at Big Black River, was defeated again and compelled to withdraw to positions already prepared in Vicksburg. On May 19 Grant ordered a general assault, but the defenders were stronger than he had expected and the attack was repulsed all along the line. Three days later he tried again only to fail a second time. The Union commander saw that he must undertake the long deliberate siege which he had hoped to avoid.

Within the city the civilian population and troops settled down to a regime of hardship that would last for several weeks. Rations soon became slim and before the end soldiers and townspeople alike were reduced to mule meat, and not much of that. Shells burst in the city at frequent intervals and much of the population took refuge in the numerous caves to be found in the steep hillsides. In many places the lines of the opposing armies were only a few yards apart and any soldier careless enough to expose himself became the victim of sharpshooters.

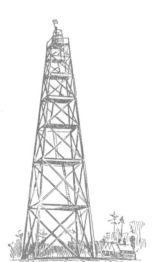

Signal tower before Petersburg, Va.

128

By early July it was evident to Pemberton that he could hold out no longer and that he could not expect relief from the army of Joseph E. Johnston several miles away. On July 3 Pemberton sent a flag of truce to Grant proposing the appointment of commissioners to arrange terms of surrender. Grant replied that surrender must be unconditional but consented to meet Pemberton between the lines that afternoon. The conference ended without result, but that night Grant relented and offered to parole the men in Pemberton's army and allow officers to keep their side arms and one horse each. Pemberton accepted the terms. At ten o'clock on the morning of July 4 the Confederates stacked their arms in front of their lines. Grant had captured nearly 30,000 men, 172 cannon and 60,000 muskets. More important was the control of the Mississippi River, now open to Union commerce and troop movements throughout its entire length, following the fall of Port Hudson, Louisiana, four days later.

Grant marks Independence Day by the capture of Vicksburg

In the last days of the siege of Vicksburg, a battle equally important was fought in and around the town of Gettysburg, in Pennsylvania.

After his victory at Chancellorsville, Lee decided to invade the North a second time. His reasons are not entirely clear but it is probable that he hoped to encourage the defeatist feeling which was becoming a force of importance in the North and perhaps to influence at least some of the European powers to recognize the Confederacy. In any case his troops would find forage, food, and supplies in the rich country of southern Pennsylvania.

Volck pictured prayer at the headquarters of Stonewall Jackson, mortally wounded at Chancellorsville.

*Lt. General John C. Pemberton,
defender of Vicksburg. Because
he was a native of Pennsylvania,
Pemberton was unjustly suspected
of disloyalty to the South.*

Lee's advance units started west and north from Fredericksburg on June 3. Hooker, aware that Lee had some kind of movement in mind, kept close watch. As the Army of Northern Virginia moved northward, Hooker put the Army of the Potomac on a parallel course to the east, thus shielding the populous cities of the East Coast. After three weeks, when Lee was in southern Pennsylvania and Hooker behind him in northern Maryland, the Federal commander was relieved by a disenchanted and disgusted President Lincoln. General George Gordon Meade, a corps commander, was immediately put in his place.

Only three days later advance units of the two armies stumbled into each other at Gettysburg, a few miles north of the Maryland line. On July 1 the Federal cavalry commander, John Buford, reconnoitering ahead of the army, encountered Confederate infantry advancing from the northwest. Buford, recognizing the strategic importance of the position, dismounted his outnumbered troopers and determined to stand his ground until Federal infantry could come up. Among the first to arrive was the famous Iron Brigade, black-hatted veterans from Wisconsin, Michigan, and Indiana. Two-thirds of its 1800 men were lost in a futile effort to hold Seminary Ridge, an elevation west of the town. By the end of the day the Federal troops had been driven through Gettysburg, but had taken up strong positions on Cemetery Ridge, parallel with and a mile and a half east of Seminary Ridge.

On July 2 Lee determined to attack. Longstreet was to strike

130

Meade's left, or south flank, in the main assault; Ewell and Early were to engage the Federal right and center to prevent Meade from shifting troops to that part of his line which Longstreet would be attacking. The Confederate advances could not be got under way until late afternoon, and then they were poorly co-ordinated. The men fought gallantly but made no lasting gains.

After the firing died away on the night of July 2, Lee had a decision to make. On the first day of the battle the Army of Northern Virginia had driven back the Army of the Potomac. The second day, just ended, had been a stalemate. The Confederate commander could hold his ground and wait for Meade to attack. He could admit failure and start withdrawing to Maryland and Virginia. Or he could make one more assault on the Federal lines. With unlimited faith in his troops, this was the course he took.

Mayor Mayo was unduly concerned. The Union was concentrating all available forces in pursuit of Lee in Pennsylvania.

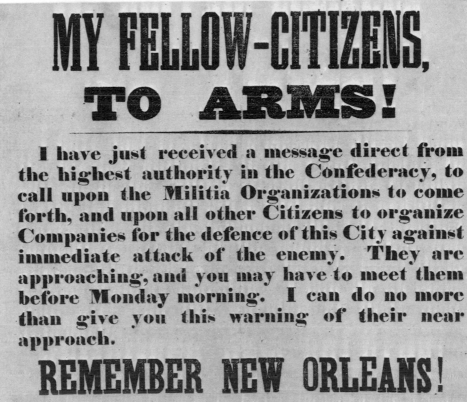

MY FELLOW-CITIZENS, TO ARMS!

I have just received a message direct from the highest authority in the Confederacy, to call upon the Militia Organizations to come forth, and upon all other Citizens to organize Companies for the defence of this City against immediate attack of the enemy. They are approaching, and you may have to meet them before Monday morning. I can do no more than give you this warning of their near approach.

REMEMBER NEW ORLEANS!

Richmond is now in your hands. Let it not fall under the rule of another BUTLER. Rally, then, to your Officers to-morrow morning at 10 o'clock, on BROAD STREET, in front of the CITY HALL.

JOSEPH MAYO,
Mayor of Richmond.

Saturday Afternoon, June 27, 1863.

CHICAGO HISTORICAL SOCIETY

A postwar view of Gettysburg

As a striking force Lee chose the fresh division of George E. Pickett and two divisions commanded by James J. Pettigrew and Isaac R. Trimble, both severely punished in the fighting of the last two days. Having tested both flanks, this time Lee would hit the Union center. After an artillery duel that lasted two hours—the greatest demonstration of its kind in the entire war—Longstreet, with the utmost reluctance, ordered the advance. In intense heat 15,000 veterans moved forward steadily across open fields and toward the crest of the slope where Federal guns stood wheel to wheel and the blue infantry lay behind low stone walls. The Union artillery cut gaps, but the steady lines closed up without faltering. At close range the Federal infantry discharged a volley, then fired at will. The Confederates charged to the wall and for a few minutes fought fiercely with bayonets and clubbed muskets. But the odds were too great. The gray wave broke, and the survivors, with the wounded who were able to walk, straggled back to Seminary Ridge, from which they had taken off. There Lee rode from one group to another, speaking words of consolation and encouragement, and admitting to one dejected officer: "All this has been *my* fault—it is *I* that have lost this fight."

In Washington, elation at the victory gradually turned to disappointment. Meade had not pursued Lee as the Confederate commander drew back to the Potomac. The fact was that both armies had been badly mauled. Even the victorious Army of the Potomac was in a state of exhaustion and confusion. Meade finally decided upon pursuit, but when he found the Confederates strongly entrenched he decided against an attack and permitted Lee to cross the Potomac

Signal tree-top

Major General George Gordon Meade, who succeeded Hooker in command of the Army of the Potomac three days before the battle of Gettysburg

on the night of July 13. Lincoln never recovered from his disappointment that Meade had been content to drive the Army of Northern Virginia from Union soil instead of grasping the opportunity of destroying it.

In more than two years of war Vicksburg and Gettysburg were by far the most important Union victories. Ironically they were followed by the most violent outburst of disloyalty that the Union had to contend with. Disaffection in the North had been growing for many months. Thousands of people were disturbed by what they considered to be the dictatorial acts of the Lincoln administration—the suspension of the writ of *habeas corpus,* the imprisonment of dissenters without trial, and the suspension, usually quickly revoked, of newspapers which opposed the government. Other thousands resented the Proclamation of Emancipation. They had been willing enough in the beginning to fight for the Union, but they had no stomach for fighting to free the slaves. The cost of living rose steadily, bearing hardest upon the poor. Worst of all from the standpoint of many thousands was the conscription law, which went into effect in the spring of 1863. Young men of means could buy exemption by paying $300 for a substitute, a sum that was far beyond the reach of any laboring man. People affected

On the spare wheel

133

Lieutenant General James Longstreet, C.S.A.
At Gettysburg he was sullen and lethargic.

by all these disadvantages wanted the war to come to an end and cared little whether the North or the South was victorious.

Disloyalty simmered most dangerously in New York City. There, in spite of many warnings of trouble, Federal authorities undertook to put the draft into effect on July 13. A mob comprised mainly of foreign-born laborers attacked the draft headquarters and burned and pillaged stores, hotels, saloons, even residences. Police, firemen, and the local militia failed for four days to restore order. Not until the government sent in picked troops from the Army of the Potomac did the mob subside. During the riots property worth $1,500,000 was destroyed and no fewer than one hundred five people, many of whom were Negroes, lost their lives. A month later drawings for the draft took place without disorder.

Riots, North and South, disclose the war-weariness of people behind the lines

Dissatisfaction with the way the war was going was not limited to the North. Three months before the New York draft riots a mob in Richmond, composed mostly of hungry women, broke into provision stores to seize meal and flour. The disturbance grew and the rioters, now joined by many ruffians, engaged in general pillage. Governor Letcher sent troops to the scene and threatened to order them to fire on the mob if it did not disperse. "If he had done so," one observer commented, "he would have been hung."

The situation became so menacing that President Davis appeared, mounted a dray and pleaded with the rioters. According to a government official, "he urged them to return to their houses, so that the

134

Meade's headquarters at Gettysburg

House next to Lee's headquarters at Gettysburg

Major General
George E. Pickett.
With Pettigrew, Pickett
led the hopeless attack
on the Union center
at Gettysburg.

bayonets there menacing them might be sent against the common enemy. He told them that such acts would bring *famine* upon them in the only form which could not be provided against, as it would deter people from bringing food to the city. He said he was willing to share his last loaf with the suffering people . . . and he trusted we would all bear our privations with fortitude, and continue united against the Northern invaders, who were the authors of all our sufferings. He seemed deeply moved; and indeed it was a frightful spectacle, and perhaps an ominous one."

Similar outbreaks occurred in Augusta, Columbus, and Milledgeville, Georgia; in Salisbury, North Carolina; and in Mobile, Alabama.

But lawless disturbances behind the lines happened too infrequently to affect the conduct of the war. In the same summer of 1863 that Grant tightened his hold on Vicksburg, and Meade defeated Lee at Gettysburg, Rosecrans, commanding the Union's Army of the Cumberland, finally moved against Bragg and the Confederate Army of Tennessee. In a masterful campaign of maneuver the Federal commander pushed the Confederates back to Chattanooga with very little loss of life. However, this important railroad center and supply depot was heavily fortified and its reduction would not be easy. Rosecrans divided his army into five groups and decided to encircle the Tennessee town and bag the Confederates gathered there. Bragg, seeing the danger, withdrew to a strong position in northern Georgia and from there planned to attack Rosecrans' forces and defeat them piecemeal before they could come together. Rosecrans frantically concentrated

In Tennessee,
Union forces push back
the Confederates

136

Chickamauga, September 19–20, 1863. A drawing by A. R. Waud.

his army. On September 19 the two forces clashed in the rolling, wooded ground along Chickamauga Creek. All day the battle surged with neither side gaining any permanent advantage. That night Longstreet arrived with a heavy reinforcement from the Army of Northern Virginia. On the following morning the Confederates attacked again, driving back the Union forces except for the left wing commanded by George H. Thomas. On that day Thomas won the sobriquet he carried for life, "The Rock of Chickamauga." During the afternoon Rosecrans, believing that his troops had been hopelessly defeated, left the field for Chattanooga and ordered a general retreat. Thomas remained behind protecting the Federal rear. Bragg did not realize that he had won a major victory, failed to follow the retreating Union army, and let the chance of destroying his enemy slip from his fingers.

In Chattanooga, Rosecrans found his army besieged. The Confederates controlled the sources of supply and the Union troops went on half-rations. Although he had been an able commander until he panicked on the second day of Chickamauga, and although he had not

Carrying a log

137

General Braxton Bragg, C.S.A. He did not realize that he had won at Chickamauga.

Major General George H. Thomas, U.S.A. On September 20, 1863, this forty-seven-year-old Virginian won the soubriquet "The Rock of Chickamauga."

lost the confidence of his troops, Rosecrans was relieved of his command a month after the battle and Grant was put in charge. At the same time two corps of the Army of the Potomac were sent west under Hooker.

Grant soon succeeded in opening the supply lines and in making the Army of the Cumberland an offensive force. By November he was ready to move against the Army of Tennessee. Bragg's troops occupied positions which he considered impregnable. Several thousand men held Lookout Mountain, the precipitous peak a few miles south of Chattanooga and the Tennessee River. The major part of the Confederate army was strung along the sharp, steep bluffs of Missionary Ridge, which extended for several miles southeast of Chattanooga. On November 24 Hooker attacked the Confederates on Lookout *At Lookout Mountain* Mountain in what turned out to be a light engagement. To everyone's *and Missionary Ridge,* surprise his men advanced up the steep slopes and drove the de-*Union troops win* fenders from their positions. The following day Grant's troops *spectacular victories* formed long lines on the level ground below Missionary Ridge. Mid-afternoon brought an order to advance and to take the first line of Confederate rifle pits. The work was done in a few minutes. Without orders, and to Grant's consternation, the attacking troops continued up the steep, wood-covered slope. As they reached the crest the defenders broke into panic and ran for safety. Bragg, Breckinridge,

138

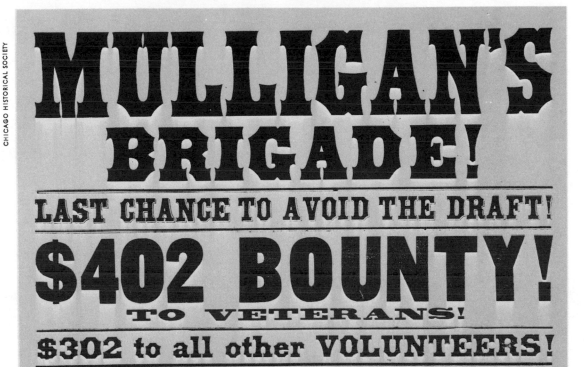

MULLIGAN'S BRIGADE!

LAST CHANCE TO AVOID THE DRAFT!

$402 BOUNTY!

TO VETERANS!

$302 to all other VOLUNTEERS!

All Able-bodied Men, between the ages of 18 and 45 Years, who have heretofore served not less than nine months, who shall re-enlist for Regiments in the field, will be deemed Veterans, and will receive one month's pay in advance, and a bounty and premium of $402. To all other recruits, one month's pay in advance, and a bounty and premium of $302 will be paid.

All who wish to join Mulligan's Irish Brigade, now in the field, and to receive the munificent bounties offered by the Government, can have the opportunity by calling at the headquarters of

CAPT. J. J. FITZGERALD

Of the Irish Brigade, 23d Regiment Illinois Volunteers, Recruiting Officer, Chicago, Illinois.

Each Recruit, Veteran or otherwise, will receive

Seventy-five Dollars Before Leaving General Rendezvous,

and the remainder of the bounty in regular instalments till all is paid. The pay, bounty and premium for three years will average $24 per month, for Veterans; and $21.30 per month for all others.

If the Government shall not require these troops for the full period of Three Years, and they shall be mustered honor out of the service before the expiration of their term of enlistment, they shall receive, UPON BEING MUSTERED O the whole amount of BOUNTY remaining unpaid, the same as if the full term been served.

J. J. FITZGERALD.

Chicago, December, 1863.   Recruiting Officer, corner North Clark & Kenzie Stree

By the end of 1863 bounties for enlistment had
gone up again. Mulligan's Irish Brigade had
been in the field since June, 1861.

"Hurrah without the H"

Grant (left) at Lookout Mountain after it was taken by Union troops on November 24, 1863

and other ranking officers barely escaped capture. The Confederate commander confessed with chagrin that "panic which I had never before witnessed seemed to have seized upon officers and men, and each seemed to be struggling for his personal safety regardless of his duty or his character." Jefferson Davis, too, blamed the defeat on the cowardice of the Confederate troops. Two weeks after Missionary Ridge he would write, in his annual message to his Congress: "After a long and severe battle, in which great carnage was inflicted on him [the enemy], some of our troops inexplicably abandoned a position of great strength, and by a disorderly retreat compelled the commander to withdraw the forces elsewhere successful, and finally to retreat with his whole army to a position some twenty or thirty miles to the rear."

Nevertheless, not even Davis could save Bragg, long a personal favorite. A week after Lookout Mountain and Missionary Ridge, the Confederate President turned over the command of the Army of

140

ONE MONTH MORE
FOR BOUNTIES

A few more Recruits can yet be received for the

FIRST CHICAGO BOARD OF TRADE
(72nd ILL.) REGIMENT!

Men of Illinois, this is the last opportunity that you will have of enrolling yourselves in the glorious army that your State has sent into the field for the defense of the Union. The forward movement of our armies, in the Spring, can but crush into powder the remaining power of this miserable Rebellion.

COME FORWARD, THEN!
AND FORM A PART OF THE TRIUMPHANT HOST!

$302 BOUNTY
TO NEW RECRUITS!
$402 to Veterans!

To any person who will bring an acceptable Recruit to my office, a cash premium of $8, or a certificate entitling him to $15 after the recruit is mustered into the service, will be paid.

Office with ESQ. POND, South-East corner of Public Square. Galesburg, Ill.

D. W. WHITTLE, Captain 72nd Regiment Ill. Infantry.

The 72d Illinois, raised in July 1862,
had fought valiantly at Vicksburg.

Tennessee to Joseph E. Johnston, whom Davis disliked with an intensity which only the overwhelming necessities of the Confederacy could surmount.

While the western armies were stalemated in the interval between Chickamauga and the battles of Lookout Mountain and Missionary Ridge, the Union had a diplomatic triumph in England. The same Confederate agent, James Bulloch, who had succeeded in acquiring and equipping the commerce raiders *Alabama* and *Florida,* had also contracted through third parties with the Laird Brothers, an English shipbuilding firm, for the construction of two ironclad ships which were believed to be capable of breaking the Union blockade. It was soon apparent to Charles Francis Adams, United States Minister to England, that the ships were intended for the Confederacy. Adams made repeated representations to the British authorities that the construction of the ironclads and their release would be a violation of English neutrality that would call for the most severe reprisal of which the United States was capable. For a time it seemed as if the British intended to ignore the protests of the American minister. But on the eve of the delivery of the ironclads to the intermediaries of the Confederacy, the British acted and the ships were not allowed to leave port. Bulloch reported sadly: "No amount of discretion or management on my part can effect the release of the ships." Thus balked, the Confederacy could no longer hope for aid from Europe.

Edwin Forbes pictured a winter camp, Army of the Potomac, in late January, 1863.

A. R. Waud sketched Burnside's disastrous "Mud March" on January 20–23. After this fiasco Burnside was relieved of the command of the Army of the Potomac.

Burial grounds grew in number and size as the war dragged on. Edwin Forbes sketched one of hundreds.

"The Gallant Pelham." As a major in Jeb Stuart's horse artillery he was killed at Kelly's Ford, Virginia, March 17, 1863. Three Southern girls are said to have put on mourning after his death.

Heavy guns in Fort Sumter. Oil painting by Conrad W. Chapman.

Fort Sumter as it appeared from Fort Moultrie. Oil painting by Conrad W. Chapman.

Fort Moultrie, manned by Confederate troops in 1863.
An oil painting by Conrad W. Chapman.

Fort Sumter, December, 1863, battered but defiant. The fort
withstood strong Federal attacks on April 7 and September 8,
1863. Oil painting by Conrad W. Chapman.

The house in which Stonewall Jackson died, May 10, 1863

Brigadier General Benjamin H. Grierson, U.S.A. His daring cavalry raid, in April, 1863, prepared the way for Grant's campaign against Vicksburg.

Throughout the siege of Vicksburg many of the inhabitants took refuge in the numerous caves within the city. This is A. J. Volck's conception of cave life.

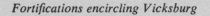

Fortifications encircling Vicksburg

An 1876 view of the Chancellor house

Vicksburg. General John A. Logan's headquarters.

Pleasonton's Union cavalry charging Jeb Stuart's Confederate horsemen at Brandy Station, Virginia, June 9, 1863. In this engagement the Union cavalry demonstrated for the first time that it could meet the Confederate cavalry on equal terms.

Vicksburg after its surrender, July 4, 1863

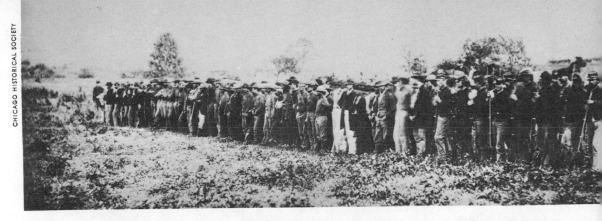

An engagement at Fairfax Courthouse, Virginia, on June 27, 1863, as Lee's Gettysburg Campaign moved toward its climax, was a Confederate victory. But the defeated Federals took prisoners.

Union wagon park at Brandy Station after its evacuation by Confederate forces

Two Union cavalry commanders who proved their competence in 1863: Brigadier General George A. Custer and Major General Alfred Pleasonton. Both served in the Army of the Potomac.

Dead horses in one segment of the Gettysburg battlefield

Union dead on the second day's field at Gettysburg. Usually the shoes were gone. They were prized by the poorly supplied Confederates.

A part of the human harvest at Gettysburg: Federal dead.

Little Round Top, Gettysburg, bitterly contested but successfully defended by Union forces on July 2

A Confederate sharpshooter who picked off his last man at Gettysburg

Railroad cut west of Gettysburg, where the two armies came together on July 1, the first day of the battle

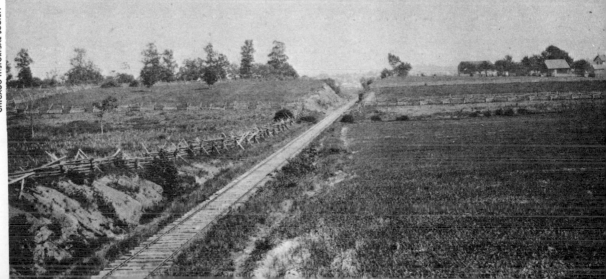

Another Confederate sharpshooter caught in the rifle sights of a sharp-eyed opponent

"Children of the Battlefield." A carte-de-visite photograph found in the pocket of a sergeant of the 134th New York Volunteer Infantry, killed at Gettysburg. The photograph was sold for the benefit of the children.

Confederate prisoners taken at Gettysburg

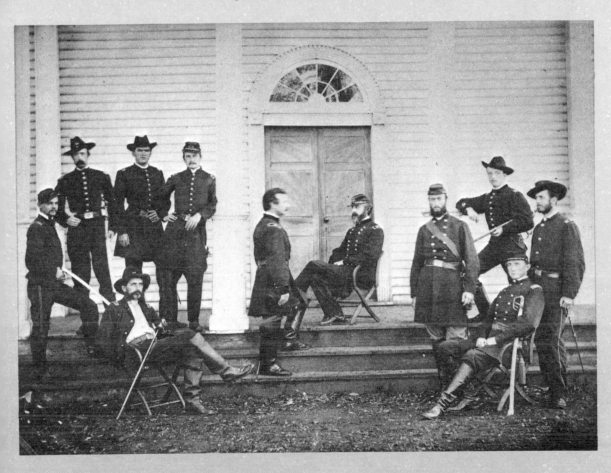

Major General George Gordon Meade, victor at Gettysburg, and his staff at Culpeper, Virginia, 1863. Meade is seated in front of the doorway.

153

*A bit of the action at Chickamauga, September 18, 1863,
caught by A. R. Waud in an unfinished wash drawing*

*Lee and Gordon's mills at Chickamauga, sharply con-
tested on September 19, the first full day of battle*

Brigadier General James A. Garfield. As a member of Rosecrans' staff this future President of the United States contributed to the defeat at Chickamauga.

John Burns, resident of Gettysburg and veteran of the War of 1812 and the Mexican War, fought with Union troops throughout the three days of the battle.

In September, 1863, while Bragg and Rosecrans maneuvered before the battle of Chickamauga, Charles Francis Adams, U.S. Minister to Great Britain, persuaded Her Majesty's government to impound two powerful ironclad rams built for the Confederacy. It was a greater victory than many of those which cost thousands.

Union officers and their friends on Lookout Mountain, overlooking the
Tennessee River, after Hooker's spectacular victory on November 24

Union military hospital built on Lookout Mountain after its capture

*Chattanooga, Tennessee, a prize fought for by
both armies in the summer and fall of 1863*

*The state capitol
at Nashville, Tennessee,
a Union stronghold
after its capture in 1862*

*As yet they were free
only as they followed
the Union armies invading
the South. Edwin Forbes
painted these fugitives in oil.*

*The camera caught
the Negroes
more realistically.
These two had attached
themselves to
a Union military unit.*

Attendants at a U.S. military hospital at Nashville in 1863. Or were they camp followers?

The railroad depot at Nashville, 1863

The H. L. Hunley, C.S.N., painted here by C. W. Chapman, was a true submarine with an eight-man crew. The Hunley *drowned three crews, seventeen men in all, before she sank the Federal sloop* Housatonic *on February 17, 1864. Both ships went down in the encounter.*

By an act of March 3, 1863, the Union provided for the conscription of able-bodied men to fill up its armies. Any drafted man could escape service by paying $300 or furnishing a substitute. Brokers in substitutes did a thriving business, satirized here by A. J. Volck.

On November 19, 1863, President Lincoln dedicated the military cemetery at Gettysburg. John Hay, the President's secretary, wrote that "the procession formed itself in an orphanly sort of way & moved out with very little help from anybody." The procession is shown here.

One of the basic facts of army life: army bread, or hardtack. Even young men with strong teeth had to boil or fry this flint-like substance before they could eat it.

A Confederate torpedo boat, known as a "David," painted by C. W. Chapman. On October 5, 1863, this boat attacked the armored Federal ship New Ironsides, *and after inflicting some damage on its target, sank.*

A field headquarters of the U.S. Christian Commission, which provided stores, clothing, tracts, and stationery to the soldiers

Newspaper vendors, welcome visitors to the armies

Quasi-official photographers accompanied the armies— in this case Sam A. Cooley, Department of the South.

Punishment: a thief being drummed out of the army at Morris Island, South Carolina, in July, 1863

Confederate soldier, 1863, as sketched by F. H. Schell. He still had a presentable uniform.

STATE DEPARTMENT OF ARCHIVES AND HISTORY, RALEIGH, N.C.

This Confederate, also sketched by F. H. Schell, was far more typical. By 1863 most Confederates in the ranks wore butternut homespun instead of gray worsted.

163

By the end of 1863 the war had lasted more than two and a half years. Small wonder that Winslow Homer gave the title "Home Sweet Home" to this painting of two pensive Union soldiers.

164

UNION ARMIES
SLUG THE SOUTHLAND

T HE WINTER OF 1863–64 turned out to be especially cold. The principal armies lay in their camps in the west around Chattanooga, in the east in Virginia north of the Rappahannock, waiting for the renewal of battle in the spring.

After the victories at Chattanooga, the Congress of the United States passed a bill to revive the grade of lieutenant general in the army. This high rank had been conferred on only two men in the country's history —Washington, who held it for a short time at the end of his life, and Scott, on whom it had been conferred by brevet only. It was generally understood that with the revival of the grade Grant would be nominated. The bill passed in February, 1864, and Lincoln immediately sent Grant's name to the Senate. The nomination was confirmed within a week and Grant was ordered to report to Washington as soon as possible.

Grant reached the capital on the evening of March 8. That night there was a reception at the White House. Grant appeared while the reception was still in progress and met the President for the first time. The crowd, too excited to be restrained by etiquette, broke into cheers. Grant, blushing with embarrassment, had to stand on a sofa so that all could see him. An hour passed before he could escape from the admirers who pressed forward to shake his hand.

*Ulysses S. Grant, still wearing
the stars of a major general, as he
appeared in Washington to receive a
lieutenant general's commission*

The next day, in a formal ceremony, the President presented the general with his new commission. Both men made short talks. "As the country herein trusts you," Lincoln said, "so, under God, it will sustain you. I scarcely need to add that with what I here speak for the nation, goes my own hearty personal concurrence." Grant replied: "It will be my earnest endeavor not to disappoint your expectations. I feel the full weight of the responsibilities now devolving on me; and I know that if they are met, it will be due to those armies, and above all to the favor of that Providence which leads both nations and men."

On March 12 Grant was placed in command of all the Union armies. Even before the order was published he had started west to confer with Sherman about the movements which he hoped would bring the war to an end.

Grant laid down a grandiose but essentially simple strategic plan. As soon as the roads were dry Sherman, with the western armies, would move on the Confederates under Johnston with Atlanta as his objective, thus preventing Johnston from reinforcing Lee. Grant

Trestle bridge, No. 1

would accompany the Army of the Potomac, still under the command of Meade, in a drive against Richmond. Both armies were to take off as early in the spring as conditions permitted.

The eyes of the North focused on Tennessee and Virginia, but many thousands of men stood under arms elsewhere. One such place was Fort Pillow, on the east bank of the Mississippi River forty miles north of Memphis. The fort had been built originally by the Confederates, but had been occupied by Union troops since the early summer of 1862. In April, 1864, its garrison consisted of one regiment of loyal Tennesseeans and four companies of Negro artillery—557 men in all. On April 12 Nathan Bedford Forrest, a former slave trader who had come to be a cavalry commander of real genius, attacked the fort with 1500 men. After several hours he succeeded in surrounding it. Under a flag of truce he sent a demand for the garrison's surrender. The demand was refused. Forrest attacked immediately. After a short period of sharp fighting the garrison fled toward the river. Forrest's men pursued the defenders relentlessly, killing many. Throughout the North, Forrest was accused of murdering helpless men after they had surrendered. Newspapers called for reprisals against Southern prisoners. Lincoln, not too sure of the facts, and unwilling to abrogate the rules of so-called civilized warfare, outrode the storm of criticism. To this day Fort Pillow is the subject of argument. That many helpless men were put to death is certain, but defenders of Forrest point to the fact that of the 336 survivors, 226 were unhurt or only slightly wounded, which would not have been the case had there been anything truly approaching a massacre.

Fort Pillow: Did Forrest's men massacre the Negro garrison?

Several hundred miles southwest of Fort Pillow, an ambitious Union venture bogged down in one of the worst military fiascoes of the war. Early in the year Halleck had assembled a force which he put under the command of Nathaniel P. Banks to invade Louisiana, Arkansas, and Texas. The country was rich with cotton which could be seized and sold for the benefit of the Union. Moreover, a successful foray into this part of the South would serve as a warning to the French that their effort to put the Austrian Archduke Maximilian on the throne of Mexico would not escape the attention of the United States when its hands were freed.

For the expedition, Halleck drew troops from several sources and put together a substantial army. In co-operation with Banks, Admiral D. D. Porter was ordered to take a powerful fleet of gunboats up the Red River. The destination was Shreveport in northwestern Louisiana.

Banks usually performed ineptly except for his capture of Port Hudson, Louisiana, in July, 1863. In this campaign he ran true to form. One contingent of his command did not reach him until he was already in trouble, while another never even came close to his army. A sharp

Trestle bridge, No. 2

*Major General Nathaniel P. Banks,
who barely escaped complete disaster
in the Red River campaign*

engagement twenty miles from Shreveport stopped him from advancing
farther. At the same time he encountered a natural obstacle that he
could not surmount. For April, the Red River was at an unusually
low level and falling steadily. Porter saw that if he did not get his
gunboats away very soon he might lose them all in Red River mud.
Reluctantly Banks turned his army about and headed back for its point
of departure. The gunboats had a hard time and succeeded in escaping
only because of an ingenious system of dams that an army engineer
devised. Late in April the expedition reached the Mississippi. Part of
the troops were sent to Sherman, and Banks turned the remainder over
to General E. R. S. Canby, who had recently been given command of
the Union forces west of the Mississippi.

By early May the roads had dried in Virginia and the Army of the
Potomac was once more in fighting trim. On May 4 Grant put it in
motion, thus beginning a campaign which he confidently expected

Corduroying

A typical section of the Wilderness, May, 1864

would end the war. That night his men camped on the edge of the Wilderness, an expanse of stunted trees and underbrush almost impenetrable, not far from the old battlefields of Fredericksburg and Chancellorsville. The next day Grant found Lee and the Army of Northern Virginia blocking his way. For two days men struggled almost in blindness. Often the opposing forces could not see each other. Cavalry were useless, and cannon, if they could be moved into position at all, were dragged in by the men themselves. Casualties were heavy on both sides.

After repulses of this kind, other Union commanders had given up. Not Grant. On May 7 he planned to turn Lee's right flank and move in the direction of Richmond. For five days fighting swirled about Spotsylvania Court House, a crossroads which the opposing commanders considered vital. The fight culminated on May 12 in a savage struggle for a position which has gone down in history as the "Bloody Angle." A Union officer wrote: "It was chiefly a savage hand to hand fight across the breastworks. Rank after rank was riddled by shot and shell and bayonet-thrusts, and finally sank, a mass of mutilated

169

Rescuing wounded from forest fires in the Wilderness.
A drawing by A. R. Waud.

corpses; then fresh troops rushed madly forward to replace the dead, and so the murderous work went on. Guns were run up close to the parapet, and double charges of canister played their part in the bloody work. The fence-rails and logs in the breastworks were shattered into splinters, and trees over a foot and a half in diameter were cut completely in two by the incessant musketry fire." The cruelest feature of the battle was the forest fires which broke out from time to time, taking the lives of many of the wounded who could not be carried away by their comrades.

Grant again refused to give up. In fact, on the day before the Bloody Angle, he had sent his famous message to Halleck: "I propose to fight it out on this line if it takes all summer." For several days the two armies sparred in the vicinity of Spotsylvania. Then Grant decided on another turning movement which Lee parried in bloody fighting on the North Anna River. By this time he could anticipate Grant's tactics. To forestall the Union commander, Lee took up strong positions in the vicinity of Cold Harbor, on the Chickahominy River ten miles

170

northeast of Richmond. Here Grant made the biggest mistake of the campaign, perhaps the biggest mistake of his military career. On the night of June 2 he ordered a frontal attack at dawn on the following morning. Officers moving along the Federal lines noticed men pinning pieces of cloth or paper with their names and home addresses onto the backs of their coats. As veterans they knew that casualties would be heavy and they were preparing their own identifications. The attack, which began on schedule, lived up to the expectations of those who had been ordered to make it. In a half hour the Army of the Potomac lost 7000 men, killed or wounded, against Lee's losses of no more than 1500. Even Grant admitted that no advantage compensated for his heavy loss.

One day after Grant began his campaign against Richmond, Sherman moved out from Chattanooga. Under his command he had the Army of the Cumberland, the Army of the Tennessee, and the Army of the Ohio—98,000 men and 250 guns. In his path at Dalton, Georgia, twenty-five miles to the southeast, stood Joseph E. Johnston with the Army of Tennessee. His position, screened by mountains, was a strong one. Sherman, thoroughly familiar with the terrain, had no intention of attacking the Confederate troops. Instead he planned to

Barlow's division in a suicidal charge at Cold Harbor, June 3, 1864.
Drawing by A. R. Waud.

slip around them to Resaca, fifteen miles south of Dalton. Johnston declined to fall into the trap, moved backward fighting as he went, and made Sherman's slow progress as costly as possible. However, it was progress. By early June the two armies faced each other only twenty-five or thirty miles northwest of Atlanta.

With Grant taking tremendous losses in Virginia, and with Sherman still short of his objective and opposed by a Confederate army which its commander had kept intact, the first moves in the presidential campaign of 1864 took place. (The Confederate Constitution provided for a six-year presidential term, so the Confederacy did not this year have to stand the stress of a nationwide election.) On May 31 a small segment of the Republican party—extreme radicals who wanted no more of Lincoln under any circumstances—assembled at Cleveland. Wendell Phillips expressed the sentiment of those present, although he himself was absent, when he wrote that he regarded the Administration "as a civil and military failure, and its avowed policy ruinous to the North in every point of view. . . . If Mr. Lincoln is re-elected I do not expect to see the Union reconstructed in my day, unless on terms more disastrous to liberty than even disunion would be." In one day the Cleveland Convention adopted a platform and nominated John C. Frémont for President. Lincoln, informed that 400 had attended the Cleveland gathering, reached for his Bible and after a moment's search read these words: "And every one that was in distress, and every one that was in debt, and every one that was discontented, gathered themselves unto him; and he became a captain over them: and there were with him about four hundred men."

The Republican party, taking the name of National Union party in the hope of attracting to itself a substantial number of War Democrats, assembled at Baltimore on June 7. Many of its leaders would have been happy to supplant Lincoln and had been intriguing for several months with that purpose in mind. But the President's hold upon the masses was too strong. On the second day of the convention he was nominated on the first ballot with only the Missouri delegation, under instructions to cast its 22 votes for Grant, opposing him. When the roll call was completed, the Missouri delegates changed their votes and made the nomination unanimous. The convention dropped the Vice President, Hannibal Hamlin, and nominated in his place the War Democrat, Andrew Johnson, Military Governor of Tennessee.

The Democrats, whose National Convention had also been scheduled for June 7, postponed it until late summer. They were well aware of the strong dissatisfaction with the progress of the war that existed in many parts of the North and decided to play for time in the hope that a summer of military frustration would work to their advantage.

For this hope there seemed to be an adequate basis. Nowhere was

Part of the cost of Cold Harbor. A burial party at work there in 1865.

the war going well and in some places, from the standpoint of the Union, it was going very badly. One of these was northern Mississippi and southern Tennessee. There Forrest continually harrassed the Union forces. To dispose of the aggressive Confederate cavalryman, Sherman ordered General Samuel D. Sturgis to fit out an expedition at Memphis, corner Forrest, and destroy him. Early in June, Sturgis started with 9000 men, a force three times the size of Forrest's.

Nature refused to co-operate. Rains turned roads into mud and sent the creeks out of their banks. Sturgis called a council of war but refused to accept the advice of his officers that the expedition be dropped. Only a few weeks earlier the Union commander had been forced to abandon a similar mission, and his pride would not allow him to confess a second failure. On June 10 Sturgis and Forrest collided at Brice's Crossroads in northern Mississippi 100 miles southeast of Memphis. From the beginning the battle was bungled by the Union command. Troops became entangled with their supply train, guns were mired in the mud, and the whole conflict turned into a wild melee. On the night of the tenth, Sturgis could not even be found, so the senior officers decided on retreat. For miles they had to fight off Forrest's horsemen. Ambulances loaded with sick and wounded were left behind. By the time the Union force made good its escape it had lost nearly one fourth of its number, and Forrest was as free as ever for his hit-and-run attacks.

173

The end of the Confederate raider Alabama, *June 19, 1864*

Shortly after the Brice's Crossroads disaster the Union would win an important victory, although word of it would not reach the United States for several weeks.

Since slipping away from Liverpool in the mid spring of 1862, the Confederate raider *Alabama* had sunk, burned or captured more than sixty merchant ships. For two years she had evaded the men-of-war sent against her. In June, 1864, John A. Winslow, Captain of the U.S.S. *Kearsarge,* caught the *Alabama* in the harbor of Cherbourg, France. Her commander, Raphael Semmes, who seems to have been living in the age of chivalry, sent word to Winslow that if he would wait until the *Alabama* took on coal she would come out and give battle. On the morning of June 19 she emerged and headed for the *Kearsarge,* lying seven miles offshore. The *Kearsarge* mounted seven guns, somewhat heavier than the eight the *Alabama* carried. Neither ship was ironclad although the Federal commander had hung rows of heavy chains over the side of the *Kearsarge* to protect her engines. When the *Alabama* came within a mile, the *Kearsarge* fired the first shots. The two ships narrowed the gap between them, circling around

Double-turreted monitor

a common center. The *Kearsarge* soon demonstrated its superiority. After an hour and ten minutes the *Alabama* began to sink. Semmes struck his flag and his men took to their boats. Most of them were rescued by the *Kearsarge* and by an English yacht in the vicinity. The gravest threat to Federal commerce sank to the bottom of the English Channel.

Grant's troops had been so badly hurt at Cold Harbor that he was unable to resume the offensive immediately. When he did he decided to give up the direct approach to Richmond, move around that city to the east, take Petersburg, twenty-five miles south of the Confederate capital, and then strike north. In the middle of June he executed the movement so skillfully that for critical hours Lee did not know the whereabouts of his opponent. The fortifications in Petersburg were lightly held. The attacking Union troops, overconfident, went about their work with little dash. Beauregard, in command of the defenses, brought in all the men he could and held off the attackers. Three days later Lee arrived, and the Federal forces had to admit that the town could not be taken. Grant was as reluctant as he had been at Vicksburg to settle down for a long siege. In that state of mind he authorized an attempt to breach the Confederate lines by means of a mine. A Pennsylvania regiment consisting mostly of coal miners ran a tunnel 500 feet, at the ends of which they placed four tons of powder. The explosion was set for 3:30 on the morning of July 30. The hour came. Nothing happened. Two men entering the tunnel found that the fuse had burned out. It was replaced and the explosion took place at 4:40, blowing a great mass of earth into the air and carrying with it timbers, guns, and men. Union troops, deployed so as to enter the Confederate lines through the crater, were slow in attacking and were handled with disgraceful incompetence. Instead of rushing through the breach, they piled up in the hole itself where many were killed or captured. The Crater, as it came to be called, was an egregious failure. Grant now knew that only a long and bitterly contested siege would reduce Petersburg and open the way to Richmond.

Beauregard gives the Confederacy a ten months' reprieve

In Georgia, Sherman seemed to have reached an impasse similar to that in which Grant found himself. Late in June he had faced Johnston in a strong position on Kennesaw Mountain, twenty-five miles northwest of Atlanta. Sherman lost his patience. He would not go on forever flanking his wily opponent only to see him retreat relatively unhurt to another strong position. This time the Union commander would attack the Confederate position. On June 27 he sent his lines forward. They attacked impetuously but lost 2000 men in a short time.

Sherman learned his lesson. For the rest of the campaign he would

Gunboat

Lieutenant General John B. Hood, C.S.A.,
who replaced Johnston at Atlanta in July, 1864

maneuver Johnston out of his positions even if by these tactics he failed to destroy the Confederate army.

At Richmond, Lee knew that he could not break Grant's grip by any direct attack. He believed, however, that if he sent a substantial force north to threaten Washington, Grant might be forced to dispatch a sufficient number of troops to the defense of the capital to weaken his besieging lines. Late in June, Lee ordered one of his corps commanders, Jubal A. Early, down the Shenandoah Valley in the direction of Washington. As Early progressed he levied tribute in supplies and money. On July 9, at a point on the Monocacy River, thirty miles from the capital, General Lew Wallace interposed with a small force. His defeat was certain, but he held up Early long enough for Grant to send troops. Although Early had reached the line of defending forts and could see the dome of the Capitol plainly, he knew that he had arrived too late and had no choice but to retreat. Lincoln, visiting the forts, was under fire for the first and only time of the war.

Back in Georgia, Sherman, outside Atlanta, heard important news. Jefferson Davis had replaced Johnston with John B. Hood. Hood had a reputation. He was aggressive to the point of rashness and Sherman knew that he could expect a Confederate attack. It came on July 20, aimed at Thomas's troops strung along Peachtree Creek north of the city. Hood was repulsed with heavy losses. Two days later he struck again in bitter fighting which again ended in his withdrawal to the city of Atlanta.

A few weeks later the Union won a spectacular success in Mobile Bay. Mobile was one of the few ports that remained open to blockade-runners and was therefore a Union target of prime importance. In the early summer the Federal Navy Department put together an expedition of four ironclads and fourteen wooden ships and gave the command to tough old Farragut, who had proved at New Orleans that fortifications on land had no terror for him. Mobile was defended by two strong forts, Gaines and Morgan, on both sides of the three-mile channel into the Bay, as well as by an ironclad ram and three wooden gunboats. Farragut lashed himself to one of the masts of his flagship, the *Hartford,* and took a place in the attacking column. The action began at 7:07 A.M. on August 5. Within a half hour one of the Federal ships struck a mine and sank, a misfortune to which Farragut responded with his famous order: "Damn the torpedoes! Full speed

A section of the Confederate defenses at Atlanta, July, 1864

Major General William Tecumseh Sherman. With the capture of Atlanta he became the idol of the North.

ahead!" In the course of the battle the Confederate ram, the *Tennessee,* was disabled and surrendered. By ten o'clock the Federal ships were safely past the forts, which were invested by ground forces. Fort Gaines surrendered on August 7, but Fort Morgan held out until the twenty-third.

The nation's attention now shifted from the battlefields to Chicago, where the Democratic National Convention tardily convened on August 29. The party strategy which put off the convention in the hope that war weariness would work in favor of the Democrats had not been wholly successful. Grant had failed to take Richmond during the summer, and Atlanta had not yet fallen, but the imminent capture of that city was apparent to everyone. The Union had by no means won the war, but its prospects appeared to be better than they had been in the early summer. The Democrats, nevertheless, adopted a platform which declared that "after four years of failure to restore the Union by the experiment of war, during which, under the pretense of a military necessity, or war power higher than the Constitution, the Constitution itself has been disregarded in every part . . . , the public welfare demands that immediate efforts be made for a cessation of hostilities with a view to an ultimate convention of the States, or other peaceable means to the end that at the earliest practicable moment peace may be restored on the basis of the Federal union of the States." The convention then proceeded to nominate George B. McClellan for President and George H. Pendleton for Vice President. The platform was more than McClellan could stomach, so in accepting the nomination a few days later he repudiated it. In his letter of acceptance he wrote: "The Union must be preserved at all hazards. I could not look in the face of my gallant comrades of the army and navy, who have survived so many bloody battles, and tell them that their labor and the sacrifice of so many of our slain and wounded brethren had been in vain, that we had abandoned that Union for which we have so often periled our lives." By this forthright letter McClellan atoned for many of his failings.

1864: The Democrats prefer peace to victory

Democratic chances of victory were greatly impaired as soon as the National Convention of the party adjourned. Around Atlanta,

Farragut's flagship, Hartford, *stripped for action at Mobile Bay*

Pennsylvania troops voting in the field, October, 1864.
Sketch by William Waud.

Sherman had been gradually extending his lines until he threatened to cut the one remaining railroad south of the city and thus isolate it. Hood saw that his situation was critical and evacuated the city on the afternoon of September 1. Sherman took possession of the town the next day. It was a Union victory of the first magnitude.

While Sherman was bringing this first phase of his invasion to a conclusion, another Union general, P. H. Sheridan, was engaging in one of the most successful campaigns of the war. Lee's Army of Northern Virginia had long depended upon the fertile farms in the Shenandoah Valley for food and forage. Grant now decided to put an end to this source of supply. He felt strong enough to detach Sheridan with nearly 50,000 men and instructions to devastate the valley thoroughly. In a letter to Halleck written a few weeks earlier Grant had declared his purpose "to eat out Virginia clear and clean . . . , so that crows flying over it for the balance of this season will have to carry their provender with them." To oppose Sheridan, Lee sent Early with some 25,000 men.

For several weeks Sheridan went about his business almost un-molested. By early October he could write that he had destroyed more

180

than 2000 barns filled with wheat, hay, and farm implements, over 70 mills, and that he had driven off more than 4000 head of stock and had killed and issued to his men at least 3000 sheep. But he was not to complete his mission unopposed. On September 19 Early, overconfident, attacked Sheridan at Winchester and suffered a sharp defeat. Three days later the two armies met again in the battle of Fisher's Hill and again Sheridan won the day.

A Union party (Republican) election poster appealing to Northern Democrats to vote for Lincoln and Johnson

A SOUTHERN PEACE!

DEMOCRATS!

BE NOT DECEIVED WITH THE IDEA THAT THE REBEL LEADERS WILL WILLINGLY CONSENT TO A RESTORATION OF THE UNION.

In the Rebel Official Report of the interview between JEFFERSON DAVIS and MESSRS. JAQUESS and GILMORE, DAVIS dismissed them with the declaration—

"THAT THE SEPARATION OF THE STATES was an accomplished fact; that he had no authority to receive proposals for negotiation except by virtue of his office as President of an Independent Confederacy; and ON THIS BASIS ALONE must proposals be made to him."

In his last message to the Rebel Congress, JEFFERSON DAVIS, in speaking of peace, describes

"THE ONLY PEACE POSSIBLE BETWEEN US—a peace which, recognizing the impassable gulf which now divides us, may leave the two people separately to recover from the injuries inflicted on both by the causeless war now waged against us."

In a Speech to the Legislature of Mississippi, Dec. 26, 1862, JEFFERSON DAVIS said—

"AFTER WHAT HAS HAPPENED the last two years, my only wonder is, that we consented to live so long a time in association with such miscreants. Were it ever proposed to enter again into a Union with such a people, I could no more consent to do it than to trust myself in a den of thieves."

DEMOCRATS! Are you prepared to legalize Secession, to recognize the Independent Sovereignty of the States, and thus to perpetuate Revolution and Civil Strife? If not, Vote for LINCOLN and JOHNSON, and thus secure the only sure Peace.

A frenzied portrayal of Sherman's March to the Sea.
From an engraving after a painting by F. O. C. Darbey.

Sheridan had expected that these two victories would end the Confederate resistance in the valley. Early, however, obtained reinforcements, reformed his army and on October 19, while Sheridan was in Winchester, attacked the Federal troops at Cedar Creek. The attack was a surprise and successful in the first hours of the battle. Sheridan, at Winchester on his way back to his troops, learned of the fighting and rode madly to the front. There he found thousands in a disorganized retreat. Rallying them, he ordered a counterattack. This time it was the Confederate ranks which broke. Early's defeated forces retreated. The Shenandoah Valley would be of no more use to the Army of Northern Virginia.

The capture of Mobile, the fall of Atlanta, and Sheridan's victories in the Shenandoah Valley put a different face on the presidential election. As late as August 23 Lincoln himself had believed that he would not be re-elected. That day he had asked the members of his Cabinet to indorse a folded sheet of paper without reading it. On it he had written: "This morning, as for some days past, it seems exceedingly probable that this Administration will not be re-elected. Then it will be my duty to so co-operate with the President elect, as to save the Union between the election and the inauguration; as he will have

182

secured his election on such ground that he can not possibly save it afterwards."

In this terse and somewhat cryptic manner Lincoln expressed his opinion that the Democratic platform would force a President of that party to seek some compromise short of the unqualified restoration of the Union. But by October, when the results came in from the states which elected their officials in that month, everyone knew that Republican success was certain. The first returns to come in on the evening of November 8, Election Day, showed Republican majorities larger than even the most optimistic had expected. Before midnight it was apparent that Lincoln's re-election would be almost a landslide. When the votes were counted he had a popular majority of more than 400,000 over McClellan and carried the Electoral College by a vote of 212 to 21. He took the result without exultation. "Now that the election is over," he said, "may not all, having a common interest, re-unite in a common effort, to save our common country? For my own part I have striven, and shall strive to avoid placing any obstacle in the way. So long as I have been here I have not willingly planted a thorn in any man's bosom.

"While I am deeply sensible to the high compliment of a re-election," he continued; "and duly grateful, as I trust, to Almighty God for having directed my countrymen to a right conclusion, as I think for their

Volck, from the Southern viewpoint, saw death and destruction in the wake of the armies.

Savannah as Sherman's men saw it in December, 1864

own good, it adds nothing to my satisfaction that any other man may be disappointed or pained by the result."

The election was hardly over before Sherman put into effect a plan he had been maturing for several weeks. Ever since the fall of Atlanta he had been trying to catch and destroy Hood's forces north of the city. He had not succeeded, and had become convinced that to corner Hood was beyond the power of the troops he could spare for that purpose. Instead he would leave Atlanta, live on the country, and march through Georgia to Savannah. To take care of Hood he would send Thomas to the vicinity of Nashville and thus prevent, he hoped, the Confederate leader from carrying out a cherished plan to menace, if not invade, some of the Northern cities along the Ohio River. Grant, somewhat reluctantly, gave him the permission he sought.

Sherman marches through Georgia to the sea

On November 12 Sherman started to render Atlanta useless from a military standpoint, burning all the public buildings, foundries and machine shops, and even some residences. He had already issued his orders for the coming march. His troops were to be divided in two wings and to move eastward—he would not specify his destination— by parallel routes. There would be no supply train and they would forage for food and grain. There would be no destruction of property except that ordered by corps commanders as punishment for attacks upon the moving columns. Negroes who could be used as laborers could be taken along with the troops, but a general exodus of slaves was not to be permitted. The columns were to start at seven o'clock each morning and to make approximately fifteen miles a day.

On November 15 the advance units of Sherman's 62,000 men

Another view of Savannah. The ocean may be seen on the horizon.

marched out of Atlanta with flags flying and bands playing "John Brown's Body." Day after day they pressed across the state, meeting little opposition. Many a veteran found the march the high point of his military service. There was plenty of food, no fighting, and marches that could be made in a few hours. Before the troops had progressed far they realized that their destination was to be Savannah, Georgia's beautiful port. On December 10 Sherman reached his goal. Three days later he took Fort McAllister, south of the city, and thus established contact with Admiral Dahlgren's fleet, lying off the coast. On December 22 he wrote a telegram to Lincoln: "I beg to present you as a Christmas gift the city of Savannah, with 150 heavy guns and plenty of ammunition, also about 25,000 bales of cotton." Sherman had, in fact, taken a prize of much greater importance. With fewer than 2000 casualties he had destroyed a large portion of the war potential of the deep South, he had demonstrated that a large section of the Confederacy was a defenseless shell, and he had placed his army in a position from which he could move north and co-operate with Grant in a final campaign against Lee.

Sherman gives Lincoln a Christmas present

While Sherman was approaching Savannah, events were coming to a climax in Tennessee. There Thomas had deployed his troops in positions in the center of the state south of Nashville. Well informed of enemy movements, he knew in advance that Hood, with 38,000 men, was moving north. Thomas immediately pulled his forces together. On November 30 Hood attacked Schofield, who had not yet reached his destination, at the town of Franklin some twenty-five miles south of Nashville. The battle was desperate, with Hood attacking

185

repeatedly and recklessly. When the day ended, the Federal army held the field but slipped quietly north to join the main body of Thomas's force at Nashville.

As Hood saw the situation, he had no choice but to attack Thomas even though the latter outnumbered him and had the advantage of position. Thomas, on the other hand, was determined to attack Hood as soon as his army was reinforced, organized, and supplied. His failure to act immediately almost cost him command. Grant became impatient and petulant at the delay. In an uncharacteristic lack of understanding he sent repeated telegrams expressing his displeasure at Thomas's failure to move—treatment that the loyal Virginian, who had fought with valor and competence on many a field, did not deserve. Grant, unimpressed by Thomas's explanation that several days of freezing rain had made troop movements impossible, dispatched John A. Logan to Nashville to take over the command. By December 15, however, the frozen ground had thawed. Early that morning Thomas sent his columns forward. The Confederates fought valiantly, as they always did, but were driven back. Even then Hood hoped for success, but on the sixteenth Thomas struck again. His victory was the most overwhelming of the war, for on that day and in the several days of pursuit which followed, he literally smashed Hood's army to pieces. As a fighting force it was finished.

Union officers enjoy themselves at Brandy Station on the Rappahannock, before the beginning of Grant's campaign against Richmond.

As 1864 opened, the Nashville & Chattanooga Bridge over the Tennessee River remained in ruins. Union engineers were building a pontoon bridge.

Pontoon boat, basic element of the pontoon bridge

Opposing armies, even though inactive, often probed each other. Here A. R. Waud showed artillery fouled in mud in the course of a Union reconnaissance in force.

(UNIONIST EXTRA.)

GLORIOUS NEWS!

REPORTED CAPTURE OF

20,000 PRISON'RS

WASHINGTON, MAY 13, 1864.

Terrible fighting on Tuesday.

Glorious victory on Wednesday.

Lee driven from his fortifications. Our troops in pursuit.

Sheridan destroys railroads, and cuts Lee's communications with Richmond.

Sigel moving forward by forced marches.

Butler fighting near Petersburg, and Beauregard in Petersburg with 25,000 men. Railroads cut and seige to be commenced.

Lee asks for cessation of hostilities and is refused by Grant.

Rumored defeat of Lee, and capture of 20,000 prisoners and 12 cannon.

Premature jubilation. Eleven months would pass before these claims would be made good.

Grant: a photograph believed to have been taken at the time of the fighting in the Wilderness

Union troops crossing the Rapidan at Germanna Ford as the Army of the Potomac moved south

Mosby's Rangers returning from a raid

Officers of the partisan rangers commanded by Lieutenant Colonel John S. Mosby. These guerrilla fighters, never numbering more than 200, harassed the Army of the Potomac during the Wilderness and at many other times.

Thwarted at Petersburg in June, 1864, Grant had to resort to siege operations. A. R. Waud sketched a Union battery of 20-pounders firing on the Confederate works.

Battery A, 2d U.S. Colored Artillery, Army of the Cumberland

Negro troops took heavy losses at the Crater. This soldier was typical of those who died there.

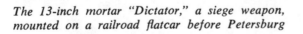

The 13-inch mortar "Dictator," a siege weapon, mounted on a railroad flatcar before Petersburg

*A spirited engraving, from a painting by J. A. Elder,
of the savage fighting at the Crater, July 30, 1864*

*Sergeant J. L. Baldwin of Company G,
56th U.S. Colored Infantry*

A Negro soldier of an unidentified regiment

Forge, Army of the Potomac, Petersburg

A "fancy" group watching a cockfight before Petersburg. At the time of the Civil War the word "fancy" was often used in the sense of "fast" or "sporting."

In June and July, 1864, the Confederate General Jubal A. Early tried to divert Federal troops from Lee's front by a raid on Washington. The capital was defended by a ring of forts like Fort Lincoln. Company H of the 3d Massachusetts Artillery is shown.

By the winter of 1864–65
the siege of Petersburg
had become grim.

Repair shop, Army of the Potomac, Petersburg

Explosion of munitions, August 9, 1864, at City
Point, Virginia, held by Benjamin F. Butler's Army
of the James. Engraved from a sketch by A. R.
Waud.

Field telegraph battery wagon,
Army of the Potomac, Petersburg

Fort Morgan, Confederate stronghold at Mobile Bay, surrendered a little more than two weeks after Farragut's victory.

An interior view of Fort Morgan

Company E, 4th U.S. Colored Infantry at Fort Lincoln

In the summer of 1864 the U.S. War Department made a strenuous effort to induce veterans whose terms were expiring to re-enlist, and to fill up the ranks of veteran regiments with new recruits.

The Lead Mine Regiment, from Grant's home town of Galena, wanted men "to rid the land of rebels."

RECRUITS

FOR THE

36TH ILLINOIS REG'T!

Now is your time to enlist in an old Regiment, that has been in the field nearly three years, and has re-enlisted for three years or during the war.

All able bodied men, between the ages of 18 and 45, who have heretofore been enlisted, and have served for not less than nine months, who shall re-enlist, will be considered as

VETERAN VOLUNTEERS,

and will be entitled to receive one months pay in advance, and a bounty and premium of $462. New recruits will receive one months pay in advance, and a bounty and premium of $302. Recruits will be allowed to select the Company which they may wish to serve in.

Each recruit, Veteran or otherwise, will receive

SEVENTY-FIVE DOLLARS

In cash before leaving General Rendezvous, $75 at the first regular payment thereafter, $50 in six months, and the remainder of the bounty in regular instalments till all is paid. The pay, bounty and premium for three years, will average $24 per month for Veterans, and $21 30 per month for all others, not Veterans, and the monthly rate of compensation will increase as the term of service is diminished. If the Government shall not require these troops for the full period of three years, and they shall be mustered honorably out of the service before the expiration of their term of enlistment, they shall receive, upon being mustered out, the *whole amount of bounty remaining unpaid,* the same as if the full term had been served.

All wishing to join the "Old 36th," can do so by calling at the Re- cruiting Station at Elgin, or the Branch Station at Bristol, Kendall County, or Crystal Lake, McHenry County.

GEORGE D. SHERMAN,

Major 36th Illinois, Commanding Recruiting Party.

This poster appeared on walls and fences in Knox County in western Illinois.

RECRUITS WANTED

FOR THE

VETERAN 45TH

ILLINOIS INFANTRY,

Washburne Lead Mine Regiment.

$402 BOUNTY AND PREMIUM

FOR VETERAN VOLUNTEERS.

$302 Bounty and Premium for New Recruits.

$75 PAID IN ADVANCE.

A Premium of $25 will be paid to any non-commiss'oned officer, private, or citizen, presenting an accepted veteran recruit, or $15 for an accepted new recruit.

Fall In, Fall In!

This is a glorious opportunity for all able-bodied Men between the ages of 18 and 45, who wish to rid the land of Rebels, to enlist in a Regiment that has passed with honor through a dozen hard fought battles, and whose Colors have never drooped in defeat.

THE

Lead Mine Regiment

Had the distinguished honor to lead the advance into Vicksburg, and their tattered old banner was the first to float to the breeze from the dome of the Court House, on that ever memorable and more than glorious 4th of July, 1863.

All particulars given as to Pay, Clothing, &c., by calling at the Office, over Gilbert's Drug Store, State St., West Rockford.

R. P. SEALY, Lieut. Col.

45th Illinois Recruiting Officer

Assisted by GILES C. HARD.

Register House Printing Establishment, Rockford, Ill.

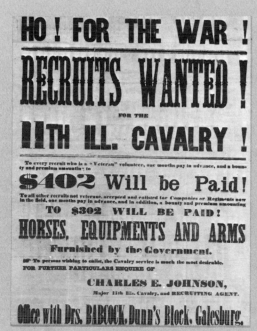

HO! FOR THE WAR!

RECRUITS WANTED!

FOR THE

11TH ILL. CAVALRY!

To every recruit who is a "Veteran" volunteer, one months pay in advance, and a bounty and premium amounting to

$402 Will be Paid!

To all other recruits not veterans, accepted and enlisted for Companies or Regiments now in the field, one months pay in advance, and in addition, a bounty and premium amounting

TO $302 WILL BE PAID!

HORSES, EQUIPMENTS AND ARMS

Furnished by the Government.

To persons wishing to enlist, the Cavalry service is much the most desirable. FOR FURTHER PARTICULARS INQUIRE OF

CHARLES E. JOHNSON,

Major 11th Ills. Cavalry, and RECRUITING AGENT.

Office with Drs. BABCOCK, Dunn's Block, Galesburg.

Peachtree Creek, where Hood hit Sherman's
army hard on July 20, 1864

Inside the Union lines encircling Atlanta in July, 1864

Working on the
Dutch Gap Canal.
It was finished
too late to be
of military value.

General Benjamin F. Butler, bottled up at Bermuda Hundred south of
Richmond, set out to dig a canal at Dutch Gap on the James River
so that he could attack Confederate fortifications at Drewry's Bluff.

The railroad station at Atlanta
after the fall of the city

A Union picket post outside of Atlanta

Engines and rolling stock captured at Atlanta

*Officers of the
82d Illinois Infantry
at Atlanta. After the
city fell the troops
had a celebration.*

*By 1864 the Union Navy had become invincible.
The* Pawnee, *shown here, was one of hundreds
of warships that kept the South in quarantine.*

Against well-manned, well-armed ships like this the Confederacy could send only a few naval improvisations.

In Philip Henry Sheridan, Major General, U.S.A., Early met more than his match in the Shenandoah Valley.

Lt. General Jubal A. Early, C.S.A. In September and October, 1864, he tried to drive Union forces under Sheridan from the Shenandoah Valley.

The Albemarle, Confederate iron-clad, was commissioned in April, 1864, and sunk by a torpedo in late October of the same year.

The U.S. Navy Department built many monitors, sometimes called rams, after the success of Ericsson's original in 1862.

The Bat, British-built block-ade-runner, was captured off Wilmington, North Carolina, October 10, 1864, on her first trip.

Gunboats, like the one in midstream, and packets (foreground) enabled the Union to dominate the Mississippi and its tributaries.

Some monitors had two turrets.

An armored Union gunboat, the Lexington,
took part in the Red River campaign.

Reveille as the Southern artist,
W. L. Sheppard, saw it

Newspapers were read avidly by the
soldiers of all armies. Sheppard caught
the absorption of the men in a Confed-
erate trench, probably at Petersburg.

A wounded Confederate cavalry officer reaches
the rear. Another Sheppard water color.

To this water color Sheppard gave
the title, "A Sad Parting."

Reveille in a Union camp. An oil painting by Winslow Homer.

Union soldiers in Butler's Army of the James, in winter quarters at City Point, could consider themselves lucky in comparison with Grant's troops at Petersburg.

Always there was the grim task of bringing in the wounded. William Waud sketched this scene in the fall of 1864.

203

For *Harper's Weekly*
Thomas Nast drew a
lively scene of Sherman's
army marching through
Georgia. Negroes followed
the troops in
embarrassing numbers.

A sketch by William Waud,
in December, 1864, shows
prisoners liberated by
advancing Union troops.

A prisoner of war on either side suffered grievously. This
oil painting, by David G. Blythe, pictured the miseries of
Union prisoners at Libby Prison in Richmond.

As the year 1864 came to its end, Charleston and Fort Sumter remained in Confederate hands. C. W. Chapman depicted a Confederate camp in the rear of the city.

Some Confederate prisoners escaped the rigors of captivity by taking the oath of allegiance to the United States. A sketch by E. F. Mullen.

Battery Rutledge, on Sullivan's Island in Charleston Harbor, still protected Fort Sumter. Another Chapman water color.

A "Quaker Battery"—logs simulating guns—in Charleston Harbor. A Chapman water color.

Chapman gave the title "Fort Sumter Interior, Sunrise, Dec. 9, 1864" to this water color.

THE END

A T THE BEGINNING OF 1865 any realist could see that the South was nearing exhaustion. Livestock on southern farms was depleted, fewer acres were under cultivation. Industry, never of first importance, was stifled and commerce disorganized. The currency was so depreciated as to be little better than worthless. Late in 1864 in Richmond a pair of boots cost $200, a coat $350, pants $100, and shoes $125. Flour stood at $275 per barrel and before the end of the war would sell at $1000. Potatoes were $25 a bushel and even turnip greens brought $4 per peck. Chickens cost $30 a pair and no beef could be found on the market.

Everywhere people resorted to substitutes. Parched corn, rye, wheat, rice, even acorns, took the place of coffee. Since the supply of blankets, uniforms, and even shoes was woefully inadequate, most Confederate troops looked like scarecrows. Running the blockade had become far more difficult, and all too often the blockade-runners brought in luxuries which could be sold at high prices rather than necessities which took more space in the holds and brought less profit.

In the Confederate armies desertion was increasing. The South was scraping the bottom of the barrel for men. As early as the spring of 1862 the government had resorted to conscription, but the law was grossly unfair and large numbers evaded it. Gangs of armed men hid

207

in the woods and mountains and defied the enrolling officers. Early in 1865 the South decided to tap its last resource—the slave—by promising freedom to those who would enlist. But the law did not go into effect until March 20, too late for it to show any results.

The North prospers in spite of the war

By contrast the North prospered, though unevenly. The wages of labor did not keep pace with the advancing cost of living. Thousands of women, and especially those with two or three children, found it impossible to live on the meager wages of a private soldier and had to depend for subsistence upon the uncertain aid from public bodies or private welfare groups. The situation of widows was even more precarious. Prices rose steadily and the value of currency dropped in comparison with gold. In the summer of 1864, with Northern fortunes at low tide, gold reached a premium of $1.85—that is $2.85 in paper money was required to buy $1.00 in gold.

Nevertheless the Northern economy was sound. Agriculture was well sustained in spite of the many thousands of farm boys in the armies. Labor-saving agricultural machines not only took their places, but in turn brought high profits to the manufacturers. Railroads kept their tracks and equipment in good condition and paid big dividends. Makers of uniforms, blankets, tents, wagons—in fact of all military supplies—found an insatiable market. In the cities places of amusement were crowded. In spite of greatly reduced immigration, the North grew—a fact which Lincoln in his annual message of December 6, 1864, deduced from election returns. "The important fact remains demonstrated," he wrote, "that we have *more* men *now* than we had when the war *began;* that we are not exhausted, nor in process of exhaustion; that we are *gaining* strength, and may, if need be, maintain the contest indefinitely."

Militarily only two theaters of war—Virginia and the Carolinas—now counted, although both North and South had many thousands of soldiers scattered in occupied towns, forts, garrisons, and camps in other regions. Lee, with approximately 50,000 men, was immobilized at Richmond by the Army of the Potomac, 110,000 strong. Fighting—conclusive fighting—could be expected as soon as the warm spring winds dried the winter's mud. In Georgia and South Carolina spring would come earlier and Sherman could be expected to start his 60,000 men north before Grant could move.

Spring, 1865, would bring a decision by force and arms

The first important action of the year was a combined land and sea operation. Fort Fisher, near the mouth of the Cape Fear River, guarded the approach to Wilmington, North Carolina, the last Atlantic port to which blockade-runners had fairly easy access. Grant ordered General A. H. Terry to put together an 8000-man force and assault the fort in co-operation with Porter's North Atlantic Squadron. Fort Fisher's garrison numbered fewer than 2000, but Bragg, now the

Confederate department commander, sent 6000 troops to occupy the peninsula north of the fort and oppose a landing there.

Foul weather hampered Porter's gunboats and transports, but the admiral started his bombardment shortly after midnight on January 12. Four hours later the troops began to land and dig in. Porter did not renew the bombardment until the morning of January 15 when Terry's troops were ready for the assault. In spite of minor setbacks his men broke the last Confederate resistance that evening and accepted the surrender of 400 defenders. To Bragg fell the humiliating duty of reporting another defeat. At 1:00 A.M. on January 16 he telegraphed to Lee: "I am mortified at having to report the unexpected capture of Fort Fisher, with most of its garrison, at about 10 o'clock tonight. Particulars not known."

In a combined land and sea operation, Union forces take Fort Fisher and bottle up the last Confederate haven for blockade-runners

Vice President Alexander H. Stephens, a realist, assessed the significance of the Confederate defeat. "The fall of this Fort," he wrote soon after the war, "was one of the greatest disasters which had befallen our cause from the beginning of the war—not excepting the loss of Vicksburg or Atlanta. Forts Fisher and Caswell guarded the entrance to the Cape Fear River, and prevented the complete blockade of the port of Wilmington, through which a limited Foreign Commerce had been carried on during the whole time. It was by means of what cotton could thus be carried out, that we had been enabled to get along financially, as well as we had; and at this point also, a considerable number of arms and various munitions of war, as well as large supplies of subsistence, had been introduced. All other ports . . . had long since been closed."

While the armies of Sherman and Grant were poised for action,

Ruins left by Sherman's army at Columbia, in mid-February, 1865

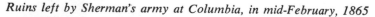

Grant, with Lee penned in Richmond, waited only for the roads to dry before forcing the Confederate commander to surrender.

Jefferson Davis agreed to a conference that only harsh necessity could have forced upon him. Francis P. Blair, Sr., the old Jacksonian Democrat who enjoyed the status of an elder statesman, saw that the collapse of the Confederacy was imminent. With Lincoln's approval Blair approached the high Confederate authorities with an invitation to meet with the President and whomever else he might choose. Davis wrote that he was willing to enter into a conference "with a view to secure peace to the two countries." After seeing this letter Lincoln expressed his readiness to bring peace "to the people of our one common country." In these two phrases lay the difference that would make the end of the war impossible until it came by military victory. Nevertheless,

210

on February 3, 1865, Lincoln and Seward met Stephens, R. M. T. Hunter, and John A. Campbell on the Union transport, *River Queen*, at Hampton Roads. Lincoln laid down three conditions for peace: (1) reunion, (2) no receding as to emancipation, and (3) disbanding of all Confederate troops. When it became obvious that the Confederate leaders were interested only in an armistice rather than the end of the war, the conference came to an end. About the only tangible result was the fulfillment of a promise that Lincoln made to Stephens during the course of the meeting. A week afterward the President wrote to his old friend: "According to our agreement, your nephew, Lieut. Stephens, goes to you, bearing this note. Please, in return, to select and send to me, that officer of the same rank, imprisoned at Richmond, whose physical condition most urgently requires his release."

An effort toward peace by negotiation fails

Perhaps it should also be mentioned that upon the break-up of the *River Queen* conference Stephens retired to his Georgia plantation, to take no further part in the government or in the conduct of the war.

The conference at Hampton Roads had met under circumstances which doomed slavery throughout the country. The Proclamation of Emancipation had touched "the peculiar institution" only in those parts of the South that were in secession when it was issued, and then only when Union troops could make it effective. To abolish slavery everywhere required an amendment to the Constitution. Resolutions to that end had been introduced in both houses of Congress in December, 1863, but while the Senate approved, the House did not. After the national elections of 1864 the prospect seemed to be far more favorable and the resolutions were introduced again. The issue was decided on the afternoon of January 31, 1865, in the House of Representa-

The remains of the new capitol at Columbia after Sherman's passage through the city

FELLOW COUNTRYMEN: At this second appearing to take the oath of the presidential office, there is less occasion for an extended address than there was at the first. Then, a statement, somewhat in detail, of a course to be pursued, seemed fitting and proper. Now, at the expiration of four years, during which public declarations have been constantly called forth on every point and phase of the great contest which still absorbs the attention, and engrosses the energies of the nation, little that is new could be presented. The progress of our arms, upon which all else chiefly depends, is as well known to the public as to myself; and it is, I trust, reasonably satisfactory and encouraging to all. With high hope for the future, no prediction in regard to it is ventured.

On the occasion corresponding to this four years ago, all thoughts were anxiously directed to an impending civil war. All dreaded it—all sought to avert it. While the inaugural address was being delivered from this place, devoted altogether to *saving* the Union without war, insurgent agents were in the city seeking to *destroy* it without war—seeking to dissolve the Union, and divide effects, by negotiation.

Both parties deprecated war; but one of them would *make* war rather than let the nation survive; and the other would *accept* war rather than let it perish. And the war came.

One-eighth of the whole population were colored slaves, not distributed generally over the Union, but localized in the southern part of it. These slaves constituted a peculiar and powerful interest. All knew that this interest was, somehow, the cause of the war. To strengthen, perpetuate and extend this interest, was the object for which the insurgents would rend the Union, even by war; while the government claimed no right to do more than to restrict the territorial enlargement of it. Neither party expected for the war, the magnitude, or the duration, which it has already attained.

Neither anticipated that the *cause* of the conflict might cease with, or even before, the conflict itself should cease. Each looked for an easier triumph, and a result less fundamental and astounding. Both read the same Bible, and pray to the same God; and each invokes His aid against the other. It may seem strange that any men should dare to ask a just God's assistance in wringing their bread from the sweat of other men's faces; but let us judge not, that we be not judged. The prayers of both could not be answered—that of neither has been answered fully. The Almighty has His own purposes. "Woe unto the world because of offences! for it must needs be that offences come; but woe to that man by whom the offence cometh." If we shall suppose that American slavery is one of those offences which, in the providence of God, must needs come, but which, having continued through His appointed time, He now wills to remove, and that He gives to both north and south this terrible war as the woe due to those by whom the offence came, shall we discern therein any departure from those divine attributes which the believers in a living God always ascribe to Him? Fondly do we hope—fervently do we pray—that this mighty scourge of war may speedily pass away. Yet, if God wills that it continue until all the wealth piled by the bondman's two hundred and fifty years of unrequited toil shall be sunk, and until every drop of blood drawn with the lash, shall be paid by another drawn with the sword, as was said three thousand years ago, so still it must be said, "the judgments of the Lord are true and righteous altogether."

With malice toward none; with charity for all; with firmness in the right, as God gives us to see the right, let us strive on to finish the work we are in; to bind up the nation's wounds; to care for him who shall have borne the battle, and for his widow, and his orphan—to do all which may achieve and cherish a just and a lasting peace, among ourselves, and with *all nations.*

From this copy Lincoln read his Second Inaugural Address on March 4, 1865.

tives. The roll call showed ayes 119, nays 56, with 8 not voting. The approval of the amendment by three-quarters of the states was assured.

Before word of the congressional action could have reached Savannah, Sherman's army started its march northward. He had hoped to leave the Southern city early in January but bad weather delayed him until February 1. The march followed the pattern of his expedition through Georgia, but where that had been something of a picnic, progress through the Carolinas presented serious obstacles. He could expect to meet much more serious opposition, for the Confederate authorities had managed to concentrate some 25,000 troops along his line of march. In addition the winter rains had come, making the poor roads almost impassable. Nevertheless, his men moved forward, averaging almost ten miles a day.

Sherman had won the enmity of the South by the march through Georgia. Now he would incur bitter and enduring hatred. As in Georgia, his men lived on the country. Foraging is at best a hardship on non-combatants, but in Georgia officers had held most of their men under reasonable restraint. In South Carolina the case was different. Thousands of men in Sherman's army looked on South Carolina as the prime mover in secession and the state which had plunged the nation into four years of bloody civil war. This state, they promised themselves, would pay the price of what they considered its perfidy. When Sherman's troops reached Columbia, where the convention which passed the Ordinance of Secession had met initially, they could no longer be held in check. Columbia went up in flames. Throughout his life Sherman contended that Confederate troops who withdrew upon the approach of his own men were responsible for the holocaust, and beyond question they had fired cotton and military stores. Confederate authorities contended that the Union officers not only made no effort to check the flames, but allowed their men to spread them.

Sherman's troops devastate South Carolina

Moving north from Columbia, Sherman fought only one engagement of consequence. It was a measure of Jefferson Davis's desperation that he restored Joseph E. Johnston to command in the Carolinas on February 23. On March 19, Johnston, with 21,000 troops, attacked Slocum's wing of the advancing army at Bentonville, North Carolina, and forced the Federals back. Sherman quickly massed his entire force preparatory to a frontal attack on the Confederate army. Johnston, knowing the overwhelming strength of his opponents, retreated. With this engagement all military opposition to Sherman's troops came to an end.

Joe Johnston's small Confederate army fights its last battle

With his army at Goldsborough, Sherman left Schofield in charge and hurried to Petersburg for a conference with Grant. On March 27 and 28 the two generals met with Lincoln and Admiral Porter to co-ordinate their plans for the final campaign. At this time Lincoln

213

*On March 27 and 28, 1865, Sherman, Grant, Lincoln, and Admiral D. Porter
conferred in the cabin of the* River Queen *at City Point to co-ordinate plans for
the final campaign of the war. A lithograph from a painting by G. P. A. Healy.*

made his policy clear. He wanted the war brought to an end as quickly
and as bloodlessly as possible, and he had no desire for reprisals against
the Confederates after they had given up their resistance. On the
other hand he warned that the field commanders must restrict themselves to the military phases of the surrenders they could expect and
leave political adjustments to the civil authorities. The President had
already expressed his general policy in the address he had delivered
when he took the oath of office on March 4. On that occasion he had
said: "Let us strive on to finish the work we are in; to bind up the
nation's wounds; to care for him who shall have borne the battle, and
his widow, and his orphan—to do all which may achieve and cherish a
just, and a lasting peace, among ourselves, and with all nations."

While Sherman was returning to Goldsborough, Grant initiated the
campaign which he expected would end the war. His strategy was to
extend his lines to the west so as to cut the two railroads that still
supplied the Confederates hemmed in in Petersburg and Richmond.
On March 29 Sheridan started his columns. Lee moved quickly to
counter the threat. On April 1 at Five Forks, fifteen miles west of
Petersburg, Sheridan defeated the Confederates under George E.
Pickett. Lee saw that his position was no longer tenable and decided
to evacuate the Confederate capital. Grant, aware that his opponent's
lines were being weakened, ordered a general assault for April 2. The

214

defenders resisted with their customary bravery, giving Lee time for an orderly withdrawal and allowing Jefferson Davis and the members of his Cabinet to escape from the doomed city. On the heels of the retreating Confederate Army and government, Federal troops entered Richmond. Their first task was to restore order to a burning, plundered city. The Confederate authorities had ordered the destruction of all supplies that could not be removed. The execution of the order was an invitation to mobs to pillage. All through the night of April 2 crowds of rowdies, deserters and stragglers, many of them drunk, had smashed their way into warehouses, stores, even private residences.

The indomitable Lee saw one chance of prolonging resistance. If he could move his men to the west and the south he could join with Johnston's troops and confront Sherman on terms not too unfavorable. The first week in April, therefore, saw a race between the Army of Northern Virginia and the Army of the Potomac. Frequent fighting took place between the two forces, but on April 7 Sheridan managed to place his brigades in front of Lee's retreating army at Appomattox, sixty miles west of Petersburg. On April 8 Grant sent a note to Lee

A telegram from Lincoln to Grant, April 7, 1865: "Gen. Sheridan says 'If the thing is pressed I think that Lee will surrender.' Let the thing be pressed."

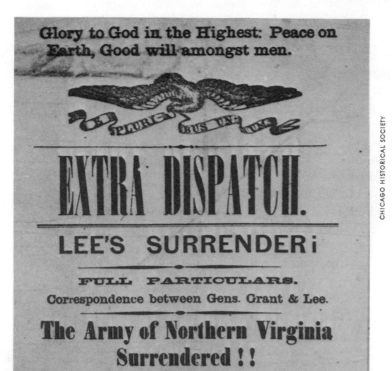

Glory to God in the Highest: Peace on Earth, Good will amongst men.

EXTRA DISPATCH.

LEE'S SURRENDER¡

FULL PARTICULARS.
Correspondence between Gens. Grant & Lee.

The Army of Northern Virginia Surrendered !!

The following correspondence concerning the most important event of the war, explains itself. It was dispatched to Gen. Pope from Was'n gton this morning:

WASHINGTON, D. C., April 9, 1865.
To Maj. Gen DODGE:

This Department has just received the official report of the surrender this day of Gen. Lee and his army to Lieut. General Grant, on the terms proposed by General Grant. Details will be given as speedily as possible   Signed
        E. M. STANTON,
            Sec'y. of War.

HEADQ'RS ARMY OF UNITED STATES, }
        April 9, 1865 P M. }
To Hon. E. M. Stanton, Sec'y of War :

General Lee surrendered the Army of Northern Virginia this afternoon upon terms proposed by myself. The accompanying and additional correspondence will show the conditions fully.

    (Signed)   U. S. GRANT,
            Lieut. General.

April 9, 1865.—General: I received your note of this morning on the picket line, whither I had come to meet you to ascertain definitely what terms were embraced in your propositions of yesterday with reference to the surrender of this army.

I now request an interview, in accordance with the offer contained in your letter of yesterday, for that purpose.

    Very resp'y, Your ob't s'vt,
    (Signed),   R. E. LEE, Gen.
To Lt. Gen U. S. Grant, Com'dg U. S A.

Your note of this date, is but this moment, 11:50 A. M. received. In consequence of my having passed from the Richmond and Lynchburg road, to the Farmville and Lynchburg I am thus writing about four miles of Walters Church and will push forward to the front for the purpose of meeting you. Notice sent to me on this road where you wish the interview to take place will meet me.

    Very respectfully,
        Your obedient servant,
        U. S. GRANT, Lt. General.
APPOMATTX COURT HOUSE, April 9, '65.
GENERAL R. E. LEE, Com'dg C. S. A. :

In accordance with the substance of my letter to you of the 8th inst., I propose to receive the surrender of the Army of Northern Virginia on the following terms, to-wit: Rolls of all the officers and men to be made in duplicate, one copy to be given to an officer designated by me, the other to be retained by such officer or officers as you may designate.

The officers to give their individual paroles not to take up arms against the Government of the United States, until properly exchanged, and each company or regimental commander sign a like parole for the men of their commands, The arms, artillery and public property to be parked or stacked, and turned over to the officers appointed by me to receive them. This will not embrace the side arms of the officers.

This done, such officer and men will be allowed to return to their homes, not to be disturbed by U. S. authority so long as they observe their paroles and the laws in force where they may reside.

    Very respectfully,
        U. S. GRANT, Lt. Gen.
H'DQRS. ARMY OF NORTHERN VA.,
        April 9, 1865.
Lt. Gen. U. S. Grant, Com'dg. U. S. A.

General: I have received your letter of this date containing the terms of surrender of the Army of Northern Virginia, as proposed by you. As they are substantially the same as those expressed in your letter of the 8th inst., they are accepted.

I will proceed to designate the proper officers to carry the stipulations into effect.

    Very Resp'y, Your Ob't. S'vt,
        R. E. LEE, Gen.

Further particulars in first Edition Evening Dispatch.

Lee surrenders!

Lee

pointing out his helpless situation and proposing that he surrender. Lee asked for terms. On the morning of the following day the two men, with their aides, met at Appomattox Court House. Grant's terms, formulated in accordance with what he considered Lincoln's policy to be, were lenient. He asked only that the officers and men of the Army of Northern Virginia surrender and give their word not to take up arms again until properly exchanged. At Lee's request Grant extended permission to the captured soldiers to take with them the horses they owned and then issued rations to the 28,000 men who were practically without supplies. The Union gunners prepared to fire a national salute; Grant forbade it. In a part of Virginia not desolated by war, where shrubs scented the air, the men of the Army of Northern Virginia stacked their arms and gave up their tattered banners in silence.

The valiant Army of Northern Virginia lays down its arms

At 12:00 noon on April 14, 1865, on the ruins of Fort Sumter, the same sergeant who had folded up the flag of the United States four years earlier handed the banner to three sailors, who fastened it to the halyards of the flagpole. Major General Robert Anderson, prematurely aged, spoke in a voice which shook with emotion. "I thank God that I have lived to see this day," he said, "and to be here, to perform this, perhaps the last act of my life, of duty to my country." Cheers greeted the flag as it rose to the top of the staff. When the shot-torn folds opened in the breeze, those who had gathered for the ceremony found release for their emotions in the familiar anthem:

> *"The star spangled banner, O long may it wave,*
> *O'er the land of the free, and the home of the brave!"*

That same night, in Washington, Abraham Lincoln with Mrs. Lincoln and a young officer and his fiancée, went to Ford's Theatre to attend a performance of the popular comedy, *Our American Cousin.* Shortly after ten o'clock, John Wilkes Booth, a popular actor driven to irresponsibility—if not insanity—by the plight of the South, slipped into the presidential box from the rear, shot the President in

Lee riding away from the McLean House after the surrender. A sketch by Alfred R. Waud.

LIBRARY OF CONGRESS

217

The McLean House, at Appomattox Court House, where Lee accepted Grant's terms for the surrender of the Army of Northern Virginia

Richmond, accidentally burned by Confederates on the eve of evacuation. The columned Confederate capitol was undamaged.

the back of the head, and leaped to the stage. Although Booth broke his leg in the jump he managed to drag himself to the stage door, mount a horse that he had kept in readiness, and make his escape.

Doctors in the stunned audience rushed to attend the stricken President. Seeing that his wound was fatal, they had him carried to a boarding house across the street. There, without regaining consciousness, he died at 7:22 on the morning of April 15.

The identity of Lincoln's assassin was quickly established and the hunt for Booth and several accomplices began at once. Ten days later he was cornered, with David Herold, a co-conspirator, in a shed near Bowling Green, Virginia. Herold surrendered; Booth defied his captors. When the shed was fired Boston Corbett, a cavalry sergeant, claimed he singled out the fugitive in the flames and shot him. Booth died three hours later.

Meanwhile another fugitive was keeping ahead of pursuers.

On the night of April 2 Jefferson Davis, two aides, and all members of the Confederate Cabinet except John C. Breckinridge, recently appointed Secretary of War, boarded a train for Danville on the last of the Richmond railroads still open. With them went the most important archives and about $500,000 in gold—all that remained of the

219

General Robert E. Lee as he waited in the parlor of the McLean House while Grant wrote the terms of the surrender. An oil painting by Thomas Nast.

treasury and all that could be found in the vaults of the local banks. The high Confederate officials left the city not only to escape capture but also to set up a new seat of government. Their trip to Danville, upon which they had settled, took twenty hours, although it was only 120 miles from Richmond. Upon his arrival Davis issued a proclamation. "I will never consent to abandon to the enemy one foot of the soil of any of the States of the Confederacy," he declared; "let us . . . meet the foe with fresh defiance, with unconquered and unconquerable hearts."

Danville remained the Confederate capital just one week. On April 10 word came that Lee had surrendered. Davis and his associates had to move at once to escape capture. This time their destination was Greensboro, North Carolina, where Johnston's army was encamped. A day after their arrival Davis and the cabinet members began a long conference with Johnston and Beauregard on the prospects of the Confederacy. Davis wanted to fight to the last man. Johnston countered that it would be the "greatest of human crimes" to continue a war when the certain result would be the devastation of the South and

On the day of Lincoln's assassination, exactly four years after the surrender of Fort Sumter, the Union flag was raised over what remained of its ramparts.

*One of several photographs taken by Alexander Gardner on
April 10, 1865, the last time the President sat for a photographer*

the ruin of its people. When only one member of the Cabinet supported
him, Davis reluctantly agreed that Johnston should ask Sherman for
terms.

Davis and the cabinet members took to the road again. Federal
troops had wrecked the railroad south of Greensboro: the refugees
had to travel on horseback and in carriages and wagons, with a cavalry
escort. By this time they had become intent upon escaping capture,
though Davis never gave up the hope that he might make his way to
Texas, where, supported by the troops under Kirby Smith, he could
prolong the life of the Confederacy indefinitely. Day by day, under
ever-increasing difficulties, the caravan moved southward. While Secretary of War John C. Breckinridge attempted to decoy the enemy,
only Postmaster General John H. Reagan remained with Davis. The
escort dwindled. Yet, in spite of the thousands of Federal troops in
pursuit, it was not until May 10 that Davis was captured near Irwin-

In this modest vault, in Oak Ridge Cemetery at Springfield, Illinois, Lincoln's body was placed on May 4, 1865.

ville, Georgia. He was immediately sent to Fort Monroe as a state prisoner.

Meanwhile Johnston had surrendered to Sherman—had, in fact, surrendered twice. Immediately after the conference with Davis and the Confederate Cabinet, Johnston asked Sherman for an armistice so that "suspension of further hostilities" could be negotiated. Sherman agreed, and suggested the Appomattox terms as the basis of a settlement. The two antagonists met near Raleigh on April 17, began discussions, and adjourned to meet again the following day. Sherman, exuberant at the prospect of ending the war on the spot, offered terms that far exceeded in generosity and scope those which Grant had tendered to Lee. In addition to providing for the disbandment of the Confederate armies—which was within his province—Sherman stipulated that the Executive of the United States would recognize the governments of the Southern states when their officers and legislatures took the oath prescribed by the Constitution; that the federal courts would be re-established; that the "political rights and franchises" of the people of all the states would be guaranteed; and that no one would be disturbed "by reason of the late war." This, clearly, was a treaty of peace, which Lincoln had forbidden both Grant and Sherman to make when he had met with them on the *River Queen*. When the text of the agreement reached Washington it was immediately rejected by President Andrew Johnson and the Cabinet, and Grant was ordered to Sherman's headquarters to direct operations against the Confederates. Grant joined Sherman on April 24. Sherman notified Johnston of the rejection of their agreement and gave him forty-eight hours in which to surrender on the same terms Lee had accepted. Johnston had no real choice. Eight thousand of his men had already started for their homes, and he believed that to prolong hopeless resistance would be criminal. On April 26 he surrendered all the Confederate forces in his command.

The Administration might have been less harsh in its rejection of the Sherman-Johnston agreement had it not been for the passions aroused by the assassination of Lincoln. Those passions were being stirred and prolonged by the funeral arrangements. On April 19 services were held in the White House and in the Capitol, where Lincoln's body lay in state. On the twentieth the long-drawn-out journey to Springfield began. In the larger cities on the route, the coffin was opened and the people were permitted to look on the face of the dead President. In every small town and village crowds gathered

The Army of the Potomac marched up Pennsylvania Avenue on the first day of the grand review, May 23, 1865.

Sherman's army nearing the White House on the second day of the grand review, May 24. These troops—the Westerners— were the idols of the spectators.

CHICAGO HISTORICAL SOCIETY

The military commission which tried the Lincoln conspirators. The presiding officer, Major General David Hunter, is second from left.

to view the somber train as it passed. Not until May 4 was the body of Lincoln lowered into its grave.

As this pageant of mourning ended, General Richard Taylor, commanding the Confederate Department of Eastern Louisiana, Mississippi, and Alabama, surrendered to General E. R. S. Canby at New Orleans. Only Kirby Smith, with the forces west of the Mississippi, remained. When Smith had learned of Lee's surrender he had breathed fire. In an order to his troops he had written: "Show that you are worthy of your position in history. Prove to the world that your hearts have not failed in the hour of disaster, and that at the last moment you will sustain the holy cause which has been so gloriously battled for by your brethren east of the Mississippi. . . . The great resources of this department, its vast extent, the numbers, the discipline, and the efficiency of the army, will secure to our country terms that a proud people can accept, and may, under the Providence of God, be the means of checking the triumph of our enemy and securing the final success of our cause." As the weeks passed Smith came to see that even in isolated Texas he could not resist the might of the

224

victorious Union. On May 26 he surrendered all the men and materiel
in his command. The New York *Tribune* headlined the news: "THE
OLD FLAG WAVES FROM MAINE TO THE RIO GRANDE!"
The announcement was not quite accurate: the Stars and Bars flew at
Galveston until June 2.

Almost coincident with the last Confederate surrender, the people
of the East had an opportunity to see and cheer the men who had
carried the banners of the Union through four tragic years. Many
thousands in Grant's and Sherman's armies remained in the vicinity
of Washington prior to discharge. The War Department ordered them
to pass in review before Grant and President Johnson on May 23 and
24. The first day was assigned to the Army of the Potomac. With
Meade at their head, the broad, carefully aligned ranks swung along
Pennsylvania Avenue from the Capitol to the White House hour after
hour. The next day came the Westerners, not so well known to the
crowds along the line of march. The cheers that greeted Sherman
testified to the place he had won in Northern regard. The ranks of
the thousands who followed him were not so neat as those the Potomac
men had presented the day before and their uniforms were often
ragged. Squads of "bummers" with donkeys loaded with spoils, and
goats and gamecocks which had become pets, delighted the crowds.

*After four years of war
the victorious armies
of the Union stage a
triumphant grand review*

*The hanging of the Lincoln conspirators, July 7, 1865. On the left, Mrs.
Surratt; the others were Lewis Paine, George Atzerodt, and Davy Herold.*

It was an informal army, but it was also the finest fighting force the world had ever seen. These men had endured the hardships of war and had seen, and participated in, its savageries, yet in a few months, without friction, they would take their places in a society at peace.

Only small raw ends of war remained. During May and June the seven men and one woman charged with conspiring to assassinate Lincoln stood trial before a military commission sitting in Washington. All were found guilty. Four—Mrs. Mary Surratt, Lewis Paine, David Herold, and George Atzerodt—were sentenced to be hanged; three were ordered to be imprisoned for life on the Dry Tortugas (the term was afterwards shortened); and one received six months in jail. The executions were carried out on July 7.

Jefferson Davis was held at Fort Monroe while Federal attorneys tried to decide what he could be convicted of. At the end of two years they gave up, and agreed that he should be released on bail. He was never brought to trial. With his discharge the Civil War receded into history.

To different people the war had different meanings. To those survivors who struggled through life without a leg or without an arm, or were harried to the end of their limited days by tuberculosis or dysentery, it had one kind of significance. To mothers and widows deprived of sons or husbands it meant sorrow, and all too often, poverty. Anti-slavery zealots found in it a cause for exultation. Southerners, returning to their plantations, and particularly to their little farms, confronted devastation and a struggle for survival. Negroes, suddenly released from slavery, tried to find their way in a world for which they had no preparation. Members of the Grand Army of the Republic and the Confederate Veterans, meeting annually and beguiled by the stirring sounds of fife and drum, came to see romance in what had been a grim lottery for survival.

A century later? One could only say that the hatreds engendered had not yet wholly subsided, and that the aspirations of men of good will had not yet been realized.

*Early in January, 1865, Sherman reviewed his
army in Savannah. Sketch by William Waud.*

*After leaving Savannah, Sherman's men had far more trouble with the mud
of winter than with the small forces of Confederates who opposed them.*

The Confederacy suffered a calamitous loss when Fort Fisher, in North Carolina near the mouth of the Cape Fear River, fell to a Union land-and-sea force on January 15, 1865. For the remainder of the war the South would have only one port —Galveston, Texas—open to blockade-runners.

Outlying gun positions of Fort Fisher. The fort had withstood a Union attack in December, 1864, but fell less than a month later.

Charleston, like Columbia, suffered at the hands of Union forces, but from the guns of an invading fleet rather than from fire.

The ruins of a Charleston warehouse as it appeared in February, 1865, when Beauregard, who commanded at the end as he did at the beginning, withdrew his troops from the city.

One of the fine old Charleston mansions battered by Union shot and shell

The "Swamp Angel," 8-inch 200-pounder Parrott rifle on Morris Island that did most of the destruction in Charleston. The gun burst on the thirty-sixth round.

Former slaves gathered at a Freedmen's Bureau headquarters at Petersburg in the summer of 1865.

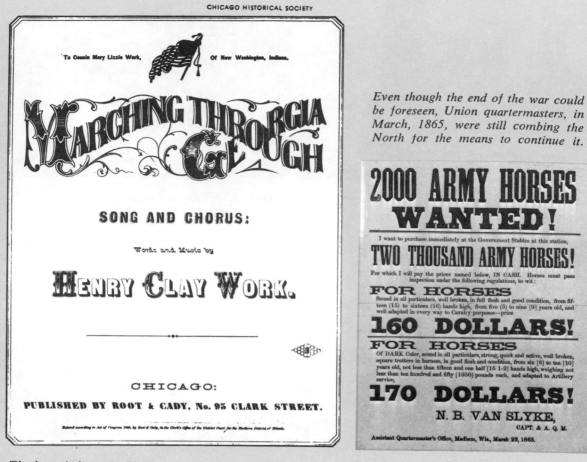

Even though the end of the war could be foreseen, Union quartermasters, in March, 1865, were still combing the North for the means to continue it.

The last of the great Union war songs. Published too late in the spring of 1865 to reach the armies in the field, it was the favorite of the bands and fife-and-drum corps of the Grand Army of the Republic to the last encampment.

The Freedmen's Bureau was set up in March, 1865, to help former slaves like these (photographed at Richmond in April) adjust themselves to a life of freedom.

Ruins of the arsenal at Richmond after the city was evacuated by its defenders

The railroad car that carried Lincoln to City Point in late March, 1865, for his last conference with Grant, Sherman, and Porter

Wharves at City Point, Virginia, supply base of the Army of the Potomac in the last months of the Civil War

With the end of the war, troops in the field relaxed—and entertained female visitors. An Illinois battery stationed at Chattanooga is shown here.

One homecoming. Lee, with his son Custis (left) and Colonel Walter H. Taylor of his staff, at his home in Richmond a few days after Appomattox.

Another homecoming: a Confederate veteran as W. L. Sheppard saw him

Ford's Theatre, on 10th Street between E and F

Laura Keene, who played the lead in Our American Cousin *at Ford's Theatre on the night of April 14, 1865*

The procession that escorted Lincoln's body from the White House to the Capitol on April 19

Chicago and Alton Railroad Company.

TIME TABLE

FOR THE SPECIAL TRAIN, CONVEYING THE FUNERAL CORTEGE WITH THE REMAINS OF THE LATE

PRESIDENT

FROM

CHICAGO TO SPRINGFIELD,

Tuesday, May 2, 1865.

Total Distance.	Dist. betw'n Stations.			
		CHICAGO	Leave	9:30 P. M.
1.7	1.7	FORT-WAYNE JUNCTION	"	9:45 "
3.5	1.8	BRIDGEPORT	"	9:55 "
12.0	8.5	SUMMIT	"	10:25 "
17.6	5.0	JOY'S	"	10:40 "
25.5	8.0	LEMONT	"	11:10 "
32.5	7.0	LOCKPORT	"	11:33 "
37.7	5.2	JOLIET	"	11:50 "
46.4	8.7	ELWOOD	"	12:18 A. M.
48.6	2.3	HAMPTON	"	12:27 "
53.0	4.5	WILMINGTON	"	12:42 "
58.0	4.8	STEWART'S GROVE	"	12:58 "
61.4	3.5	BRACEVILLE	"	1:08 "
65.0	3.8	GARDNER	"	1:22 "
74.0	9.0	DWIGHT	"	1:52 "
82.0	8.0	ODELL	"	2:17 "
87.4	5.2	CAYUGA	"	2:35 "
92.3	5.0	PONTIAC	"	2:52 "
97.8	5.6	OCOYA	"	3:09 "
102.6	4.7	CHENOA	"	3:25 "
110.6	8.0	LEXINGTON	"	3:52 "
118.5	7.9	TOWANDA	"	4:18 "
124.0	5.7	ILL. CENTRAL R. R. JUNCTION	"	4:37 "
126.0	2.0	BLOOMINGTON	"	4:43 "
133.0	6.8	SHIRLEY	"	5:07 "
136.5	3.6	FUNK'S GROVE	"	5:18 "
141.4	4.8	McLEAN	"	5:35 "
146.0	4.8	ATLANTA	"	5:50 "
150.0	4.0	LAWN DALE	"	6:03 "
156.8	6.7	LINCOLN	"	6:26 "
164.0	7.1	BROADWELL	"	6:50 "
167.6	3.7	ELKHART	"	7:03 "
173.5	5.9	WILLIAMSVILLE	"	7:22 "
178.3	4.8	SHERMAN	"	7:38 "
180.0	2.1	SANGAMON	"	7:46 "
185.0	5.0	SPRINGFIELD	Arrive	8:00 "

The following instructions are to be observed for the above train:

1. All other Trains on this Road must be kept thirty minutes out of the way of the time of this Train.
2. All Telegraph Stations must be kept open during the passage of this Train.
3. A Guard with one red and one white light will be stationed at all road crossings by night; and with a white flag draped by day, or after day-light, on Wednesday morning.
4. A Pilot Engine will run upon this time, which is to be followed by the Funeral Train, ten minutes behind.
5. Pilot Engine must not pass any Telegraph Station, unless a white flag by day, or one red and one white light by night, shall be exhibited, which will signify that the Funeral Train has passed the nearest Telegraph Station. In the absence of said signals, the Pilot Engine will stop until definite information is received in regard to the Funeral Train.
6. The Funeral Train will pass all Stations slowly, at which time the bell of the Locomotive must be tolled.

By order of BREVET BRIGADIER GENERAL D. C. McCALLUM, 2d Div., in charge of Military Railroads.

ROBERT HALE,

Time table for the Lincoln funeral train from Chicago to Springfield

The Cook County Courthouse in Chicago, where Lincoln's body lay in state from May 1 to May 2. Mourners, several abreast, are moving into the building.

A view of the Lincoln funeral procession in New York, April 25

Another view of the Lincoln funeral procession in New York. The photographer focused on the famous 7th Regiment.

Mrs. Mary E. Surratt, hanged July 7, 1865

Execution of the Lincoln conspirators, July 7. The four to be hanged were on the scaffold while the death warrant was being read.

Lewis Paine, hanged July 7, 1865

George A. Atzerodt, hanged July 7, 1865

David E. Herold, hanged July 7, 1865

Sgt. Boston Corbett claimed he shot John Wilkes Booth on April 26, 1865, in the Garrett shed between Port Royal and Bowling Green, Virginia, south of Washington. Lieutenant Edward P. Doherty was one of three officers in charge of the detail that cornered the fugitive.

Jefferson Davis's last journey. The former President of the Confederacy died at New Orleans, December 6, 1889. The body was reinterred at Richmond, May 31, 1893. Shown here: the catafalque in the reinterment.

INDEX

(References to the text are in roman type; to pictures, in italic.)